THE TRANSFORMATION PRINCIPLE

The Transformation Principle

IAN COWLEY

KINGSWAY PUBLICATIONS
EASTBOURNE

Unless otherwise indicated, biblical quotations are from the
NRSV the New Revised Standard Version, copyright © 1989 by the
Division of Christian Education of the National Council of the
Churches of Christ inthe USA.

NIV = New International Version © 1973, 1978, 1984 by the
International Bible Society.
NKJV = New King James Version copyright © 1979, 1980,
1982 by Thomas Nelson Inc.
RSV = Revised Standard Version © 1946, 1952, 1971, 1973
by the Division of Christian Education and Ministry
of the National Council of the Churches of Christ in
the USA.

ISBN 1 84291 054 X

Published by
KINGSWAY COMMUNICATIONS LTD
Lottbridge Drove, Eastbourne, BN23 6NT, England.
Email: books@kingsway.co.uk

Book design and production for the publishers by
Bookprint Creative Services, P.O. Box 827, BN21 3YJ, England.
Printed in Great Britain.

Contents

Foreword   7
Preface   11
Introduction   13

PART 1: The Church as an Agent of Change   23

As you have sent me into the world, so I have sent them into the world. And for their sakes I sanctify myself, so that they also may be sanctified in truth. (John 17:18–19)

1. The Church I Believe In   25
2. True Discipleship   41
3. A Changed World   58

PART 2: The Church that Builds Relationships   75

I give you a new commandment, that you love one another. Just as I have loved you, you also should love one another. (John 13:34)

4. The People-Centred Church   77
5. A Passion for Unity   95
6. Serving the Community and Caring for the Poor   112

PART 3: The Church Rooted in God   **127**

*'You shall love the Lord your God with all your heart, and
with all your soul, and with all your mind.' This is the
greatest and first commandment.* (Matthew 22:37–38)

7. Worship and Liturgy   129
8. A House of Prayer for All Nations   144
9. Holiness   154
    Conclusion   171

Foreword

After the tragic failure of almost the whole church in Nazi Germany to resist the rise of Hitler or to stand up for the Jews, Dietrich Bonhoeffer, imprisoned for his own part in a revolution attempted by those outside church circles, wrote from his cell prophetic words.[1] He said that the church having fought for its own self-preservation had lost its chance to speak to humanity or the world at large, thereby rendering its traditional language powerless. It would now have to remain silent and commit itself to prayer and right action until a new Christian thinking, speaking and action were to be reborn out of this right doing. By that time its form would have changed beyond recognition and *then* it would be able 'to utter the word of God with such power as would change and renew the world'.

I believe that 'new righteousness and truth' proclaiming 'the peace of God and the coming of the kingdom' even now

---

[1] Dietrich Bonhoeffer, 'Thoughts on the Baptism of DWR' in *Letters and Papers from Prison* (London, 1953).

7

can begin to be communicated wherever the church worships at that sufficient depth which is only given to it by true prayer and costly right action. I have been humbled by this discovery in the life of churches of the poor around the world. It was manifested to us in South Africa in the stand taken there by such a number of faithful Christians among others. Ian Cowley is someone whose Christian discipleship has been distinctively shaped by that South African movement. He speaks to us out of that background and he has sought to give expression to what he learnt there in his ministry here among us, as a parish priest in Britain.

I suppose at first sight, even though Ian's own church here is manifestly a church for the whole community in which it is set, it could still appear to be just one more particularly effective evangelical, charismatic Christian congregation. And there is much in this book that *could* be read as simply the credo of the successful leader of such a church. But there is a strange, radical passion running through it which is quite different. That is why for me, to enter into the worship of his church has in fact been to step into one of those vibrant places where the worship and the life of the people around you speak of that new power, a power to transform not only first and last the human heart, but also the corporate life of the church and thus of our whole Western society and world.

The transformation he is writing about is not in the end wrought by a slick technique which he can easily convey. He is not giving us a model to follow or even offering us a formula for success, a kind of prescription for making your church hum. Rather he is essentially summoning us to receive and to share a radically different attitude to life. For him the good news of Christ offers us a grace which we can only truly enter in upon through a costly commitment and a Franciscan quality of discipleship, 'the cross before us, the world behind us', which will change us profoundly within, intensifying our prayer and worship beyond recognition. It will change us into a kingdom community, requiring of us faithfulness to each other, searchingly honest and forgiving relationships, a pattern of shared and sharing leadership, a way of living which both stands out clearly from the culture around us and yet speaks to that culture and attracts many from it, especially the young of all ages. Only thus will it bring about that change in our whole world which it so desperately needs.

By contrast with the stereotype of the church many people seem to have acquired today of a rather tired, ageing and dwindling band, narrowly conventional, clinging to its past, what comes across here is something quite characteristic in my experience of many small churches and cells in the inner city and on housing estates. Or even in rural hamlets and sometimes indeed in suburbs or the kind of commuter village in which Ian's own church is set.

It is the impression of a group of people, who are quite evidently moving towards a future age, groups with a passion for justice, fired by a love which pours out of their being, to use Ian's description of Bishop Desmond Tutu, and thus always open, vital, gentle, caring and full of hope! These kinds of people are salt and light in whatever part of the world they find themselves, going out to others, appealing to the strong but also to the vulnerable, drawing into their fellowship old people, children and the young, who will join them not because of any gimmicks but because of their quality of life, their faith and their manifest integrity.

We need to learn so much more about this way of being, or rather becoming, church from Christians in other parts of the world. What imparts the strange freshness to Ian's message to us is that it comes out of that South African struggle in which he was nurtured. But essentially it is indeed 'a breath from a far country', the spiritual country of not only Desmond Tutu, but also Dietrich Bonhoeffer and Francis of Assisi. One can understand how St Francis could say, 'Preach the good news. Use words if necessary!' when one remembers that he was speaking to his brothers and sisters, whose very approach to life and to people radiated, and actually validated, the ultimate truth of their message. May this book help us to come at least a little bit closer to the grace we can share with them!

Simon Barrington-Ward

Preface

All over the world a new kind of church is emerging. It is a church that is centred on transformation and the kingdom of God. It speaks in the language and culture of the twenty-first century. It is informal and yet highly committed. Denominational barriers mean very little in this church. Instead it majors on relationships and spirituality. It cares deeply about the poor, the environment and the effects of globalisation. This is what I have called the transforming church.

Over the past two years I have been privileged to be able to travel widely and to visit churches in different parts of Europe, Africa and North America. What I have seen fills me with hope for the future of the church. From Langley Vineyard in Canada and Soul Survivor in Britain to the Diocese of Kitale in Kenya and African Enterprise and PACSA in South Africa, I have seen new models of church and mission being worked out. At the heart of this vision is the principle of transformation in the power of the risen Lord Jesus Christ.

I would like to thank with all my heart those who have

helped and supported me in the writing of this book. Among those who have given me invaluable counsel and encouragement I want especially to thank Bishop Simon Barrington-Ward, Colin Brookes, Chris Cocksworth, Bruce Collins, Malcolm Guite, Rhiannon Jones, Steve Pearson and Jonathan Strickland, as well as Graham Cray who pointed me in the right direction when the idea for this book was first taking shape. Sandra Butler and Jennie Owen have put many hours of work into typing the text. I am particularly grateful to Jennie Owen without whose help I don't think I could possibly have completed the manuscript by the publisher's deadline! I also want to thank the people of All Saints Milton for being such a loving, affirming and supportive community. This book has been written in the context of a very special local church. Thank you.

Thank you, too, to Richard Herkes and Carolyn Owen at Kingsway, who have been wonderfully positive and helpful. I thank my family, Alison, John and Grace, who know better than anyone what has been involved in the writing of this book, and have given me much space and much love, support and prayer over the past 18 months while this book has been coming into being. I could not have written it without you, so in a sense it is your book as well as mine.

Above all may this book be to the glory of God, and may he use it for the extension of his kingdom, to the honour of his holy name.

Ian Cowley

Introduction

In 1978 David Watson, the well-known British evangelist, author and church leader, wrote a book entitled *I Believe in the Church*. It was one of his most widely read and influential books, and it set the pattern for a generation of church leaders and models of ministry. But now, as we begin the twenty-first century, a new generation is emerging. The culture of the 1970s is a fading memory. A new church is required for a new culture. Many of the principles upon which David Watson based his book are still valid. But they have to be applied in new ways, and with renewed vision and commitment.

The fact is that the conventional church, as it has been known for at least the past three or four generations, is shrinking rapidly. Some would say that it is dying. Almost certainly in 20 to 30 years there will be very little remaining of the models of church life that were popular in the 1960s and 1970s. But what will take their place?

This book is a call to all who value the Christian church and care about its future to think in new ways about the shape of the church in the new century. This church will not be like the conventional church of the twentieth century, a hymn-singing, tradition-centred, formal and denominationally distinct church. The culture that supported such a model of church life is a culture that is rapidly disappearing. It is becoming as outmoded and alien as the Victorian culture was to the post-war 'baby boomer' generation. The new culture that has in many respects already taken over is informal and relaxed, where people have the right to choose for themselves, where anything goes and anyone is welcome.

So the old conventional church is making way for a new kind of church, which will not be a church that simply tries to come to terms with a changed and in many ways strange and frightening new culture. If this church is to flourish and grow it will be deeply part and parcel of the new culture, a church that belongs to it and yet is both salt and light within it. Over many years those involved in Christian missions have had to learn that before the gospel can be communicated to a new tribe or society there must be a willingness on the part of missionaries to enter into that culture, to learn the language, to win the trust of the people, and indeed to become one of them for the sake of Christ. So for some there will be the challenge of living within a rapidly changing church, a church that is itself being transformed as the culture is changing. This is not easy for many people, and for some this will simply be a bridge too far, a step they are unwilling to take. So some will battle on, seeking to keep in use the old hymns and prayer books, the old programmes and clubs, even though for the vast majority of people these are as relevant to their lives as a long-forgotten Victorian novel or even an ancient manuscript. Such things may be of great interest to particular specialist scholars or enthusiasts, but for most ordinary people they have no relevance at all.

For many others, however, the new 'postmodern' culture

and worldview is where we live out most of our daily lives. Some institutions, such as many churches, the judiciary and the universities, try to hold on to their traditions as best they can. But in many workplaces, in the media, on television and in popular music, and in much of the world of leisure, the new culture has almost completely taken over. So for many young adults, and even for many of the generation that grew up in the 1950s and 1960s, in the years of rock 'n' roll and the permissive society, it is the traditional world and the traditional church that feels alien and out of touch. Many Christians are already living out new models of church life, of worship, discipleship and mission. The church is being transformed, even as I write, and soon the church in the West will be almost unrecognisable from the conventional church of the second half of the twentieth century.

What kind of church will succeed the conventional church? I believe that already the patterns of the new kind of church are emerging all over the world. I call it the 'transforming church', as it is all about transformation. This is the church which is like the yeast in the dough, the salt on the meat, and the light in the darkness.

The culture of the twenty-first century is a culture of change, extraordinarily rapid and far-reaching change, which is constantly increasing in pace and pervasiveness. In the midst of this culture of change, the Christian church offers values and truths that are neither relative nor transient. At the heart of the Christian church lies an unchanging and eternally true gospel, the good news of God and of his love and mercy in Christ Jesus for all cultures and all generations. So the transforming church has the potential to make a very powerful impact upon the culture of change and relativism. It may even be that God will use this transforming church to turn back the tide of moral relativism in the Western world, perhaps at some time deep into the twenty-first century. But if that is to happen, the church will need to be available and obedient to Christ in some radically changed ways from those that have often been the norm in the past generation.

The transforming church is centred on transformation. God sent his Son Jesus Christ to bring transformation to every dimension of human life. Jesus is the one who alone has the power to transform the human heart, to fulfil the prophecy of Ezekiel that says, 'A new heart I will give you, and a new spirit I will put within you; and I will remove from your body the heart of stone and give you a heart of flesh' (Ezekiel 36:26).

Mark's Gospel tells us that Jesus began his ministry with a call to transformation: 'The Kingdom of God is near. Repent and believe the good news!' (Mark 1:15 NIV). The word 'repent' (*metanoia*) literally means 'change your mind', or change your ways and your approach to life. It is only through repentance that it is possible to experience the grace and forgiveness of God. As Dietrich Bonhoeffer pointed out, so often the Western church has wanted to settle for cheap grace, which is forgiveness without real change or repentance, and has thus avoided the cost of discipleship. This unwillingness to face the heart of Jesus' message has led directly to a powerless church, which has correspondingly lost much of its credibility and impact in most of Western Europe.

The transforming church takes change seriously, and this means that transformation has to begin with *me*, with each individual person who hears the call of Jesus. This means true repentance and a desire to seek costly grace, the grace that involves change and obedience and radical discipleship in the service of the Lord Jesus Christ. I believe that nothing less than this will enable the church in the West to survive in any significant form in the twenty-first century.

But a transforming church also brings about transformation. It is the salt and the light in a secular hedonistic society, the people of hope in a confused and lost generation, the community of the kingdom of God set within the kingdoms and principalities of this world.

In the past century the church has in different ways effectively proclaimed the power of the gospel of Jesus to change individual lives. People like Billy Graham and courses like Alpha have drawn many thousands to put their faith in Christ and to experience for themselves the life-changing work of the Holy Spirit. Many churches too have known the renewal of the Holy Spirit, affecting every aspect of church life. But in recent years there has emerged a growing awareness across the globe that God is in the business of transforming whole communities, and cities, and even nations. A video entitled *Transformations*, presented by George Otis Jr, has had a major impact in many parts of the world. This video describes the effect of churches working together in unity and committing themselves to fervent prayer and community action in places as diverse as Cali in Colombia, Guatemala, California and Kenya. The resulting transformation of many aspects of community life has been quite extraordinary. There has been dramatically reduced crime, growing economic prosperity and even increased agricultural productivity. Alongside the transformation of communities has come a significant rise in church attendance and a willingness of those in public office to identify openly with Christian values and standards and to look to the churches to play an active part in community affairs.

So a transforming church is not only a church that is being transformed, but one that also has a transforming effect upon the society in which it is set. Often in the past the church in the West has been divided and weak, and has been content with a one-sided view of mission, with some churches focusing on evangelism and the individual believer, and others seeing their responsibility mainly in social action and justice issues. Sometimes *neither* of these aspects of mission has been taken seriously, and mission has itself been largely forgotten.

The biblical understanding of the mission of God in Christ is that God so loved the world that he sent his only Son . . . (John 3:16). God longs for every single human being to turn and believe, that not one should perish or be lost. But he loves the world; the whole world, not just parts of it. He loves the political world, the natural world, the world of the arts, and culture, and music, and dance. He loves it all. His purpose in Christ is that the kingdom of God will break through in all the world, that it all may be redeemed and transformed, to the glory of God the creator and sustainer of all things.

At the heart of this vision of mission that is centred on transformation is something biblical and powerful – the local Christian community. The purpose of mission is surely to bring God's transforming power in Christ into our world through changed lives and changed communities. To see this happen, we must begin with the local church, or some form of basic Christian community. This community may be based around a local community or on a group or network sharing similar lifestyles, such as people who work for a certain company, or who belong to a certain age group.

The church in Britain has been so often maligned, so often seen as ineffective, out of touch, boring, weak, unfashionable. Yet God's way, as Paul tells us in 1 Corinthians 1:27, is often to choose what is foolish in the world to shame the wise. 'But God chose what is foolish in the world to shame the wise . . . God chose what is low and despised in the world, things that are not, to reduce to nothing things that are' (1 Corinthians 1:27–28).

As I read the secular media in Britain, I detect a degree of puzzlement, even exasperation, in its reporting about the Christian church. For so long now we have been told that the church in Britain is dying, that it is irrelevant and ridiculous. Equally, we are told that the Christian faith is no longer intellectually credible and that Christianity is just a crutch for weak and inadequate people.

But in spite of all this, the church has not died. Numbers of churchgoers are continuing to fall, but there are many other factors that point to the opposite of decline. In many local congregations, there is a spiritual vitality and commitment and a breadth of lay involvement unseen for generations. Church schools across the nation seem to offer something parents, even if they are not churchgoers themselves, desperately want for their children. And in countless communities, large and small, urban and rural, right across the nation, the local church continues to play a significant role.

When tragedies take place in people's lives, such as the loss of a fishing boat with all its crew, or the Dunblane shootings, it is the church and its ministers who are called upon to play a key role in enabling people to deal with what has happened. Even an event on the scale of the terrorist attacks of 11 September 2001 saw the church ready and able to provide a focus for the nation's grief. There is no doubt in my mind that in large and small ways, all over Britain, the church is touching people's lives and making a difference. Its impact and influence is far, far greater than the national media acknowledge or even understand.

In this book I shall be seeking to describe my own understanding of this vision of a transforming church and how it works out in practice. This book is, in a sense, the story of the 20 years I have spent in full-time ordained ministry and in leadership of local churches. They have been exciting, challenging, costly, and very fruitful years. As a direct result of these past 20 years, I can say that I do truly believe in a new vision for the church, a vision of a transforming church, which God will use to transform both people and nations.

Fourteen years of my ministry have been spent in South Africa, in two different churches, one where I was the assistant minister, and one where I was the rector. I have also spent ten years working in two churches in England, first as a curate in a parish in Sheffield in the north of England, and then as the rector of All Saints Church, Milton, in Cambridge. In South Africa I have seen first hand how God used ordinary people to bring about the most extraordinary change in a nation. At the forefront of this miraculous change was the Christian church. The lessons from what has happened in South Africa are, I believe, immensely important for many other nations. In particular, the church in the developed Western world has a great deal to learn from the experience of the church in South Africa.

But the church in Britain also has many strengths. It has huge potential to influence not only the nation but also to play a significant global role in the twenty-first century. Britain has for centuries been a nation from which men and women have gone out, called by God to bring the love of Christ to different parts of the earth. Today Britain is a nation with vast resources and great wealth, and a Christian heritage that God continues to use and to bless.

With a new confidence and a new vision the church in Britain can reclaim lost ground, and make a major impact on our twenty-first century world. However, this can only happen if the church is willing to obey Christ and stand for the truth, in word and deed, in a very rapidly changing world. Similarly, Christians in many other nations are finding that God is able to touch and change whole communities and cities, through a united, prayerful and obedient church.

I believe in a new vision for the church – a biblical, Christ-centred vision. It is a prophetic vision of transformation that can only become reality in our lives by the power of God, working through an obedient, servant people. But it is a vision of life, of hope, and of the kingdom of God, breaking through in new power and reality, in the world of a new century and a new millennium.

PART 1

The Church as an Agent of Change

As you have sent me into the world, so I have sent them into the world. And for their sakes I sanctify myself, so that they also may be sanctified in truth.

(John 17:18–19)

1

The Church I Believe In

I was born in Witbank, Transvaal, South Africa, in April
1951. My father worked in the coal mines at Phoenix
Colliery, near Witbank. In my early childhood we moved
every two or three years from mine to mine. I was sent to an
English-speaking boarding school in Potchefstroom in
January 1958, when I was only six years old. It was there that
I have my first memories of church.

In Potchefstroom, as I remember, there were two churches
that the English-speaking boarders could attend: Anglican
and Methodist. I came from an Anglican family and had
been christened in an Anglican church, so I went to the
Anglican Sunday school. I was initially very homesick at
boarding school, and can still remember the young woman
who was my first Sunday school teacher, and the warmth
and friendship she gave me. She was the one who first of all
welcomed me into the church. I do not remember her name,
but I owe her a great deal.

Another aspect of church life that has had a lasting impact
on my life began in the Anglican church in Potchefstroom. I
learnt to worship. I can clearly remember enjoying the hymn

The King of love my Shepherd is
Whose goodness faileth never.
I nothing lack if I am his
And he is mine forever. (H. W. Baker)

One day I asked my Sunday school teacher whether we would sing this hymn again the following week. She was surprised that a hymn like this could have made such an impression on a seven- or eight-year-old boy.

In the later 1950s my father decided to leave the mines and go farming. We moved to Natal, and I was sent to a boarding school in Pietermaritzburg, the capital of Natal province. I continued to attend church on most Sundays, because church attendance was compulsory for boarders. When I was 13 years old I was confirmed in the Anglican church, and began to receive Holy Communion.

I can clearly remember the service at St Peter's Church, in the centre of Pietermaritzburg. The priest always used the service from the old Anglican prayer book, with its extraordinarily archaic language, which he recited at breakneck speed. His sermons made no impact upon me at all. I had the overwhelming impression of the church as an outmoded and decrepit institution, stiflingly resistant to change, and hopelessly out of touch with the real world.

However, there was something that struck a chord in me. Deep down I believed in God, and without any serious questioning or understanding I believed in Jesus Christ. I found that I wanted to receive Holy Communion. Somehow in the taking of the bread and the wine, I felt that God met me, that he forgave me, and gave me a sense of peace, 'the peace that passes understanding'. Somehow in this simple act the seed of faith in me was nurtured and sustained in my teenage years.

When I left high school I was called up to do my compulsory military service in the South African army. I can remember an army chaplain giving us a lecture on the subject of 'spiritual defensibility'. He told us that when things were tough in the army, we should strengthen ourselves by remembering that we were there to fight to ensure that the white man remained supreme in our nation. Until that time I had acquired very little political awareness, even though I had been growing up through the days of Sharpeville, the Rivonia trials and the capture and sentencing of Nelson Mandela. But I knew that I was certainly not willing to serve in the South African army in order to keep the white man in power in South Africa.

I went on to enrol as a commerce student at the University of Natal in Pietermaritzburg. Here my political awareness started to grow by leaps and bounds. I joined an organisation called the University Christian Movement (UCM), and attended a number of student conferences and meetings organised by the UCM. Here I first encountered a young black student leader named Steve Biko, who at that time was involved in setting up a new black student organisation called SASO (South African Students Organisation). SASO was based on the philosophy of black consciousness, which aimed to enable black people in South Africa to shake off their dependence on whites and to take control of their own future and identity, without reference to white people. Both UCM and SASO were considered by the government to be dangerous Communist-inspired organisations. Soon I was on the local committee of UCM, and I became aware that I, together with a number of other student friends, was receiving the attention of the Special Branch of the security police. We knew who some of the local Special Branch men were; we even recognised some of their cars. They tapped our telephones; they opened our mail; sometimes they followed us in their cars as we walked down the street. A few years later I learnt that two of the five members of the local UCM committee were in fact paid security police informers. There was probably not much about my life as a student that the security police did not know.

In my third year at university I became the editor of the student newspaper, and a member of the Students' Representative Council. By now I was actively involved in local student politics, which at the University of Natal at that time almost inevitably meant that I was involved in student opposition to the apartheid system and the government. The more I learnt about the realities of life in South Africa for the vast majority of its people, the more outraged and appalled I became. I can remember for example my dawning awareness of the policy of forced removals, which was being widely implemented in Natal at that time. Close to the farm where my parents still lived was a large black community called Charlestown. One holiday I went home and they were gone. The houses, shops, churches were all standing, but the people were gone. They had been forcibly removed to a large black township near Newcastle, some 30 miles away, simply because Charlestown was regarded as a 'white' area. The cruelty, humiliation and injustice of this policy seemed indefensible to me. Yet apart from a few concerned white people, nobody I knew seemed willing to say or do anything about it. The primary reason was fear. It was dangerous to be seen to be too militant. Something bad could happen to you. You could be banned or detained; if you were black you could simply disappear.

A few months before I was due to write my final examinations, I received a clear warning from the security police. One Sunday morning at 4 am I was awoken in my room in the

Malherbe university residence. There were two security policemen standing in my room holding a search warrant with my name and address. They proceeded to search through the entire contents of my room. Every book was opened up and shaken; all the contents of my wardrobe were taken out and examined. They found nothing incriminating, and they refused to answer any of my questions. Later I discovered that I was in good company. Dawn raids had been carried out that morning against a large number of political activists, church leaders and students, including Bishop Philip Russell, the Bishop of Port Elizabeth, Athol Fugard, the playwright, and Winnie Mandela.

While my political consciousness was developing I was also moving forward in my understanding of the Christian faith. I attended both the UCM and the SCA (Student Christian Association) as well as the local Anglican church. The UCM was liberal and politically aware, while the SCA was conservative and evangelical. I was interested in finding out more about both of these expressions of Christianity. However, the UCM became increasingly disorganised and confused (probably at least in part because of the presence of so many security police agents in the organisation). The SCA on the other hand was, to me, painfully cosy and conservative. I couldn't get used to the Bible thumping, the chorus singing, and the predictability and earnestness of their meetings. Some of the SCA students came from very conservative church backgrounds. I remember one student who was convinced that the Bible clearly taught that God had made the black races to be hewers of wood and drawers of water. He believed that any church or political party that sought equality for blacks and whites was unbiblical and contrary to God's will in creation.

However, the SCA did organise annual work camps in the

'homelands' during the university vacations. Partly as a result of my problems with the security police and my responsibilities as editor of the student newspaper, I failed half of my final exams, and had to repeat the year. So the following year with the encouragement of a good friend, Pete Southey, I went to spend a week during the summer vacation at the SCA work camp at Kentani in the Transkei. Here I came to a major point of decision in my life.

I found myself deeply impressed by the missionary with whom we were working. His whole life and being seemed to me to radiate Christ. He lived very simply and sacrificially, and was filled with a genuine Christlike love for all people, black and white. After I had been there for four or five days, a day of prayer and fasting was held. I had not been used to spending a whole day in prayer, and I was not at all sure that this was something I really wanted to do. But in the course of that day I went for a walk, and in a nearby maize field I knelt down and made a decision that from that moment on I would put Christ first in my life, regardless of where it took me or what it cost.

After this I experienced a new awareness of the presence of God in my life. I started reading the Bible, even devouring it, because of the new sense that I had that God was actually speaking to me, directly and personally, through its pages. I had a real sense that I had found the truth about life, and to my amazement I had discovered that it was in the church, and among Christian people, that the truth was to be found.

Over the next two years I worked in the government Registry of Deeds office in Pietermaritzburg, and at the same time continued to study part time at the local university. It was my experience during this time that formed my convictions about the church and its role in society. For I realised in the context of South Africa in the 1970s that the Christian church could be both the agent of changed lives in the power of Jesus and the prophetic instrument God would use to change society.

These were extraordinary years. Again and again I was introduced to people who stood as examples to me of true leadership, integrity, courage and faith in Christ. They were black and white, well educated like myself or from poor rural backgrounds, male and female, young and old. They were God's new alternative society. These were the people with whom I wanted to identify, because they were the ones who, more than any other group or organisation, seemed to me to be the people who offered hope for the future of South Africa.

It is important to remember now, over eight years after the elections of 1994, just how dark and difficult those years in South Africa were. At that time it was very hard to see any light at the end of the tunnel, as the Nationalist Party's hold on power seemed unshakeable. It seemed impossible that black majority rule would come to South Africa without a titanic struggle and an accompanying bloodbath.

Yet today South Africa is a nation that has been amazingly transformed. I can now walk down the streets of Pietermaritzburg as a white South African without any sense that the colour of my skin has made me an oppressor in the land of my birth. I still find it hard to grasp that the changes of the 1990s have really happened. The South Africa I knew as a student was a place of great beauty and of wonderful people, but it was also a place of terrible suffering, injustice, inhumanity and grief. How on earth did South Africa change?

I believe that what has happened in South Africa is a miracle. What happened was not foreseen by any political commentator. There were so many times when it could all have gone so wrong, and there was such a vast legacy of hatred and injustice and pain. I am convinced that the Christian church made a critical contribution to the transformation of South Africa, through prayer, through courageous prophetic witness, and through faithful Christian service and action. Without the church, I do not believe that there would have been a peaceful election in April 1994 and the emergence of a non-racial democracy, with an ANC government led by Nelson Mandela.

The church I believe in is involved in the transformation of the world. This starts with changed hearts and changed lives, but it goes much further. If our agenda is to work and pray for the kingdom of God to come on earth, then we shall not be satisfied until this world is as God wants it to be. We shall be those who 'hunger and thirst for righteousness', and are not satisfied with anything less. There is no excuse for the church of Jesus to withdraw from the world, and limit itself to matters of personal salvation and church business. I believe in a church that brings hope and that makes a difference to the world, because God is at work in and through his people. That is what I have seen in South Africa, and that is the mission of the church in the world of the twenty-first century.

Who were those individuals who made such an impact on me in South Africa in the 1970s? Many names come to mind: Beyers Naudé, Desmond Tutu, Michael Cassidy, Edgar Brookes, Alpheus Zulu, Rob Perks, and many more. These were formative years in my life, and many incidents and impressions still remain with me. I would like to recount a few of these, because they help me to define the nature of the church that is an agent of God's transforming power.

One of the most inspiring leaders I met when in my twenties was Bishop Desmond Tutu. He was later to become

Archbishop of Cape Town and was awarded the Nobel Peace Prize for his leadership in opposing the apartheid system in South Africa. When I became Rector of a mainly white church in South Africa in the 1980s, I found increasingly that Desmond Tutu was hated by many white people. I repeatedly met white South African Christians who openly questioned whether Desmond Tutu was really a Christian. I found myself, again and again, having to defend him and what he stood for. Our church, the Anglican Church, or the Church of the Province of Southern Africa, was regarded by some as 'Tutu's church'. We lost a lot of members during the 1980s because of Desmond's uncompromising stand. It was painful for me as the rector of an Anglican church to be told that another of our church members was leaving the church 'because of Tutu'. But at the same time I was enormously grateful to Bishop Desmond for the courage of his leadership, and for doing all he could to ensure that the church of which I was a member was clearly and unequivocally opposed to apartheid.

I was able to speak about Desmond to my church members because I had come to know him personally during a small retreat he had led when he was heading the South African Council of Churches. What I remember about this retreat is not Desmond Tutu the church leader, or Desmond Tutu the voice of the voiceless. What I saw was a man so fired by the love of God that this love simply poured out of his very being. This was a man who knew God as the God who loves each person he has made, deeply and unconditionally. Desmond spoke to us about God. He said, 'God created us because he wanted to, not because he had to. Creation is the result of God's overflowing love. Creation is the object of this divine love, which was, and is, and will be, and this makes creation have an immeasurable value.'

I felt that Desmond was a man who had come to know the immeasurable love of God with an unmistakable reality and power. His words were charged with his experience of the God of love. Desmond spoke to us about how God's love was revealed to us in the incarnation, in God becoming one of us and taking the form of a servant. Desmond said to us, 'Jesus says, "I and the Father are one," and I can wash the feet of my disciples.' It all comes back to this: knowing that God loves us. 'This is as near to us as anything could be. But so often this doesn't sink into the depths of my being.'

Desmond told us, 'Friends, God loves you, from all eternity. You are not an accident. You are part of the divine plan. Every individual is unique – like the triangle in the orchestra. God desires the love of every individual. Can you accept that you are accepted? There is true freedom in this – even if your neighbours disagree with you.'

At the end of the retreat I wrote in my diary this prayer: 'God, you endow us with such infinite value. I can only fall down and worship you. Thou art God whose arms sustain the world.'

I remember asking Desmond about prayer and when he found time in his busy day for prayer. I discovered that it was his practice to get up very early in the morning to pray. He told me that he then did his intercessions in the car on the way to work. His whole life seemed to be infused with prayer. And it showed. I saw in Desmond a man who lived out his public calling as a priest and bishop in the empowering that unmistakably came from a life of intimate experience of the love of God in Jesus Christ our Lord. It was truly inspiring, intoxicating stuff. I knew that this was what I wanted to do with my life: to follow the example of a man like this. And this was the man who also said to us in this retreat, 'If our churches are comfortable, we must worry. We are called to identification with those who are suffering. The church has spoken too long from the perspective of the rich. Martyrdom means "being a witness". God has given us in this country the privilege of witnessing, and it is costly. What do you do when so many of the laws of this country are unjust? How long are we going to be mixing up what is morally and legally right?'

Another South African Christian leader who has had an enormous personal influence on my life is Michael Cassidy. Michael is a South African who was converted to Christ at Cambridge University. It was in Cambridge that Michael first had the idea of forming an organisation called African Enterprise whose aim would be to evangelise the cities of Africa. This concept developed while Michael was studying theology at Fuller Seminary in the USA, and by 1961 the dream had become a reality. I first met Michael in the late 1960s, by which time AE (as by then African Enterprise had become known) was operating from a couple of offices in Longmarket Street, Pietermaritzburg. By 1974 I too had made a commitment of my life to Christ, and I was part of a group of students who worked with Michael and a team from AE in organising a major mission to the local university. Michael had also been involved in bringing Billy Graham to South Africa, and I was trained as a counsellor for the Billy Graham mission in Durban. Indeed, much of the foundational teaching and training that I received in the Christian life, in knowing the Bible and in sharing my faith, came through the ministry of Michael Cassidy and African Enterprise.

But Michael has always been much more than an evangelist. The evangelistic ministry of African Enterprise has, since it was founded in 1961, had an enormous impact across the continent of Africa. Michael has always been committed not simply to seeing people come to faith in Christ, but in working out the wider implications of the gospel for the church and for society. For Michael, the gospel is about reconciliation, and the ministry of AE has been a ministry of reconciliation, particularly in South Africa. Michael Cassidy has been described as 'one of the great Christian strategists and communicators of the twentieth century'.[1] He has worked for over 40 years to bring Christians together and to enable them to face and work through the issues of living out and proclaiming the gospel of Jesus Christ. From the earliest days of AE, Michael was committed to a non-racial partnership of evangelists, working together to bring the love of Christ to the cities of Africa. He was deeply involved in bringing together a wide cross-section of South African church leaders, black and white, in the South African Congress on Mission and Evangelism in 1973 held in Durban. I was a young Christian student at that time, but I was there, though only for a short time. Later on, however, I participated in significant gatherings of Christians in South Africa such as SACLA (South African Christian Leadership Assembly) in 1979 and the NIR (National Initiative for Reconciliation) in 1985. In both of these gatherings, Michael's leadership was instrumental in bringing together Christians from across the spectrum of South African society and enabling them to listen to one another, to build relationships, and to begin to overcome some of the deeply rooted barriers endemic in South Africa at that time.

I also later became Michael's pastor, when I became the rector of the Church of the Ascension in Hilton, Natal, where the Cassidy family lived and worshipped. Michael has been a huge influence and inspiration in my own life. He has

---

[1] *Man of Africa* (London: Scripture Union, 1979).

shown me that the gospel is about transformation and reconciliation in every area of life. He has lived that gospel,
sometimes at enormous personal cost. He is a man of
extraordinary faith and vision, a true leader. And he is
someone who prays and listens, and is willing, again and
again, to act upon what he understands God to be saying to
him. Many lives have been changed through the life and ministry of Michael Cassidy, although I am sure that Michael
would be quick to say that it is only Jesus who can change
lives. But not only this; Michael's life and ministry have had
a significant impact upon the South African church, and
upon the nation of South Africa.

In 2001 I heard Michael Cassidy speak at a meeting in
London. He said, 'Africa is one day going to become the
fulcrum of world mission.' But Michael warned of the
danger of the church in Africa preaching 'a salvationist
message, not a kingdom message. A kingdom message is
not just salvation, but the whole of life under the rule of
God.'

I could write about many other South African Christians,
inspiring men and women of different races, languages and
backgrounds, whose lives and examples have formed my
own life, faith and vision for the church and for the world.
In closing this chapter, however, I want to honour a man
who revealed Jesus to me and to many others. His name was
Peter Kerchhoff.

I met Peter when I returned to South Africa in 1978 after
my theological training in England. I was newly ordained,
and beginning my full-time ministry in my first parish, in
Pietermaritzburg, Natal. Peter contacted me and invited me
to become involved with a new local organisation called
PACSA (Pietermaritzburg Agency for Christian Social
Awareness). PACSA was formed in order to help local

churches to grapple with the political and social realities of South Africa at that time. This was never going to be an easy task. But a small group came together and began working on a number of initiatives including the production of fact sheets on issues such as poverty, malnutrition and employment conditions for domestic workers, which we distributed to local churches. We also met regularly for support, prayer and fellowship, especially at the PACSA Agapes.

I came to know Peter as a man who had the courage to be utterly uncompromising in living out what he knew to be the way of Jesus in South Africa. Through dark and terrible days Peter continued unflinchingly to work for justice and truth, and to be a servant of the victims of apartheid. He suffered prolonged detention without trial, and he was harassed and threatened many times. He risked everything, and put his life on the line over and over again, for the sake of the poor and the oppressed.

Peter was the one who made me aware of the brutality and injustice of forced removals. He would go to the places where people were being threatened with being taken from their homes, where often their families had lived for generations. He would personally monitor the situation and try to raise awareness of what was happening. When, as so often happened, whole communities were uprooted, loaded on to trucks and taken to distant pieces of bare, windswept veld (countryside) miles from anywhere, and given a large corrugated iron drum for a home, Peter was there. He knew by name those who were suffering; they were his friends and he helped so many, often in times of great need and anguish. He was a servant of God and a man of prayer, who was ordained a deacon in the Anglican church in Natal. Yet it was only at the time of his death that many of us recognised his greatness and the extent and power of his humility.

In July 1999 I returned from England to Natal for a short visit. On the day I arrived in Pietermaritzburg I read in the local newspaper that Peter Kerchhoff had died two days earlier following a car accident. I was deeply shocked; I could hardly believe it. A few days later, however, I was able to attend his funeral at the Cathedral of the Holy Nativity in Pietermaritzburg. It was a very moving occasion, attended by a huge crowd of all races and backgrounds. Family members and friends spoke about Peter's life, his Christian work and service of so many victims of apartheid. A number of leaders and representatives from different churches participated in the service. Peter was in many ways an ordinary man, full of warmth and wonderfully cheerful and friendly, even in very difficult times. Yet in his passing he was recognised by many leaders in the church and in the community as a great man, a true servant of the people. Nelson Mandela wrote this letter to the Kerchhoff family on 19 August 1999:

I was most distressed to hear of the sudden and tragic passing of Mr Peter Kerchhoff. The wonderful work Peter has done amongst the people of our country who have suffered will always be remembered.

It is always tragic when the life of one who has done so much for others is unexpectedly taken. The manner in which Peter conducted his life is an example to all the people of this country.

I trust that you will find the inner strength necessary to face this tragedy and to continue with the great work that Peter had undertaken. South Africa has lost a son.

Please accept my sincere condolences. N. R. Mandela[1]

In September 1994 I became Rector of All Saints Church in Milton, Cambridge, in England. The challenges facing the

---

[1] Published in the PACSA Annual Report, 1999.

church in Britain are different from the South African situation during the years of apartheid. None the less there are important lessons to learn from the church in the developing world. The common enemy facing the whole Christian church in Britain is the unbelief, apathy and self-centredness of much of British society. A divided and sometimes demoralised church is making little impact on the millions who have no personal contact with or experience of the Christian church.

In South Africa we learnt that every individual person can make a difference. Change begins at the grassroots, with me and with you. But individuals have to become communities for transformation to take place. I have come to believe that the primary purpose of the church in the West at this time is to create community with Christ at the centre. Together with this we need a transformed model of discipleship, where Christians are seen to practise their faith rather than to simply give verbal assent to a set of doctrinal beliefs. Then the church can become a prophetic, transforming presence in the midst of a secular, materialist society.

2

True Discipleship

From the time when I was a university student in Pieter-maritzburg, being a Christian has for me consistently meant following a radical vision for my life, in obedience to Jesus Christ. I am drawn to a way of life that involves risk-taking and a willingness to move out of my comfort zone. I also want the truth. I don't want to settle for less than a life lived to its full potential, and it seems to me that one of the keys to this is a desire to pursue the truth in life, wherever it may take me.

When I was a student in the early 1970s, there was a lot of talk about being radical. I came to understand that Jesus is the most radical of all the revolutionaries and radicals who have ever lived. The word 'radical' comes from the Latin *radix,* which means 'root'. In our lives and in our understanding of the world, we need to try to get to the root of things. This is what Jesus is concerned about. This means a willingness and desire to seek the truth about life and about the world. Jesus said, 'I am the way, and the truth, and the life' (John 14:6). To align ourselves with Jesus is to align ourselves radically with truth, not just in our words and belief

systems, but in our actions and our lives. Christian discipleship is about the imitation of Christ. We seek the truth as it
is found in the life and teaching of Jesus, and put it into practice in our own daily lives.

The word 'disciple' comes from another Latin word
discere, 'to learn'. A disciple of Jesus is therefore someone
who is learning to be like Jesus. The goal of Christian discipleship is that we take upon ourselves the character of
Jesus more and more. To become like Jesus should be the
ultimate aim of every Christian.

This radical conviction led St Francis of Assisi to leave
behind the life of pleasure-seeking and frivolity that he had
enjoyed as a wealthy young nobleman. After a series of
dreams and visions, Francis began to live as closely as possible to the teaching of Christ in the gospel. First, he over-
came his natural disgust for lepers. One day when he was
riding near Assisi he saw a leper. By a great effort of will he
dismounted, gave the leper some money and kissed his hand.
Soon Francis was visiting all the lepers in the local leprosar-
ium, giving them money and kissing their hands. This was a
huge act of faith, but Francis did not contract the disease.
Years later, he described this experience in the opening words
of the testament that he dictated as he lay dying:

> When I was in sin, the sight of lepers nauseated me beyond
> measure, but then God himself led me into their company and
> I had pity on them. When I had once become acquainted with
> them, what had previously nauseated me became a source of
> spiritual and physical consolation for me. After that I did not
> wait long before leaving the world.[1]

---

[1] Anthony Mockler, *Francis of Assisi: The Wandering Years* (Oxford:
Phaidon, 1976).

A little while after this Francis heard the Gospel reading from Matthew chapter 10, where Jesus commands his disciples to take no bag for their journey, or two tunics, and to go out and proclaim the good news of the kingdom of God. He immediately changed his style of dress, and from that time on wore a simple, rough tunic, with a robe girdle around his waist. He learnt by heart the words of the Gospel, and aimed to put them into practice as literally as possible. For example, as Francis reflected upon the words of Jesus in Matthew 10:8–9, 'You received without payment; give without payment. Take no gold, or silver, or copper in your belts . . .', he decided to give up money altogether. From that day on he never again touched a coin or accepted gifts or payment of money.

There are many examples in history of radical Christian discipleship. In the twentieth century people such as Mother Teresa of Calcutta and Martin Luther King have lived extraordinary Christ-centred lives that have touched and inspired millions of people. There are many others who similarly have served Christ with sacrificial love, whose names will only ever be known to a few. But as we think about such men and women, many of us will find ourselves asking, 'How radical can we be?' Is it realistic to talk about taking the teaching of Jesus absolutely literally? Surely Francis of Assisi was going beyond what Jesus would normally expect of us when he refused to accept gifts of money. Was this really what Jesus intended?

Should we rather be looking for a middle way that is not as radical as Francis, but still costs us something? Or is that a convenient compromise, which enables us to escape from the demands of true obedience to Jesus?

It is interesting to notice that Jesus himself did not water down the terms of discipleship to those who found his demands hard to take. The rich young ruler in Luke chapter 18 asked what he had to do to inherit eternal life. After Jesus had spoken to him about the commandments, he said to him, 'There is still one thing lacking. Sell all that you own and distribute the money to the poor, and you will have treasure in heaven; then come, follow me' (Luke 18:22). We are told that when he heard this he became sad, because he was very rich.

In another passage, Luke 9:57–62, we hear about three would-be followers of Jesus. All of them made excuses as to why it was not convenient for them to follow him at that time. One said to Jesus, 'I will follow you wherever you go.' Jesus said to him, 'Foxes have holes, and birds of the air have nests; but the Son of Man has nowhere to lay his head' (Luke 9:58). Nothing more is heard of him. We are left to assume that the cost of discipleship was too great for him. Interestingly, Jesus did not say to him, 'Look, it doesn't have to be that bad. I'm sure we can come to some arrangement that won't be quite so difficult for you.' Jesus set out his terms, and quite plainly he wants nothing less than our whole being: my heart, my life, my *everything*.

The Spirit of truth

The call of Jesus to each individual will always be a radical call. It is a lifetime's journey, a wrestling and a struggle in which we find that God himself is working within us to lead us into all truth (John 16:13). This is what Jesus told us the Holy Spirit would do.

Harry Williams has written:

When the Holy Spirit leads us into all truth, he will be, as Christ said, within us, not outside; within the whole of us, and not just the Sunday-best part of us – the times when we feel pious and decent and pure in heart. For, as far as we are concerned, the chief work of the Holy Spirit is to reconcile what I think I am with what I really am, what I think I believe with what I really feel; to liberate what fear compels me to suffocate, to introduce the me I loathe and fear and cut dead, to introduce this very me to the glorious liberty of the children of God.[1]

It is important to grasp that true discipleship is not about a new set of religious rules and regulations we have to obey if we want to be truly Christian. That is legalism. Jesus does not call us to a new law we have to obey at all costs. His way is the way of grace and love and freedom. Jesus said, 'If you continue in my word, you are truly my disciples; and you will know the truth, and the truth will make you free' (John 8:31–32). His service is perfect freedom, says the Anglican prayer book. In serving and following Jesus we find our true selves. We are set free from those powers and inner demons that enslave us and prevent us from being the people God created us to be. The way of Jesus is liberation. It is the way of love, fully and openly embraced and lived out. It is the greatest calling that any of us can ever accept and follow.

Seduced by the world

The problem for many Christians in the West is that we have been seduced by the world. We are so enthralled by the world and all it has to offer that we find it difficult to consider giving it all away in order to follow Jesus. We want both the world and Jesus, but that is not a bargain he offers us.

---

[1] H. A. Williams, *The True Wilderness* (London: Collins, 1965).

'"Take the world, but give me Jesus" is my cry' says Matt Redman in a worship song we often sing in our church. But life in the postmodern world is all about keeping our options open, and having a pick-and-mix approach to faith and lifestyle. This is the age of self-help spiritualities that appeal to the consumer in us. We can easily become 'consumer Christians', ready to try anything that offers to add value to our lifestyle or increase our happiness and well-being.

Much of Western Christianity has already to a greater or lesser extent 'sold out' to the prevailing culture. Faith is regarded, even by many Christians, as an essentially private matter. Going to church is seen to be primarily about receiving God's blessings and peace and forgiveness. Examples of genuine radical discipleship among contemporary church leaders are rare. The prophetic cutting edge of the church in the West has largely disappeared.

What is missing is a credible Christian spirituality based on actions not words. A major bookstore in Cambridge has recently held a number of workshops and seminars promoting various New Age and Eastern spiritualities, covering topics such as 'spiritual parenting', astrology, reiki and Indian head massage. I asked them why there was nothing at all on Christian spirituality. 'These events are organised by the staff from the bookshop,' I was told. 'Nobody has suggested that we do anything on Christian spirituality, but if somebody wanted to do something that would be fine.'

Christian spirituality does not even register in the thinking of those outside the church. How on earth can this be, when the Christian faith has produced such great men and women of God as St Augustine, St Francis of Assisi, St Benedict, St Teresa of Avila, even Mother Teresa of Calcutta? We have an extraordinary wealth of tradition and experience in the history of Christian spirituality. These were men and women who had a profound effect upon their own times and cultures. They were people of transformation, because of the power and integrity of their discipleship. These were men and women who had the courage to stand against the tide of their own times. By the power of their own lives and examples they called the church and the world back to the values of Christ and the kingdom of God.

There is no doubt in my mind that it is this uncompromising quality of discipleship that changes the world. Words alone are of little value, especially in our age of information overload. It is deeds not words that count. It is how Christians live that will enable the Christian faith to take hold of the hearts and lives of people in the postmodern Western world. The future of the Christian church in the West depends upon the rediscovery of true discipleship. True discipleship has a transforming impact upon society, because it is radical in returning to the life and example of Jesus. What is needed is nothing less than a new desire to find ways of fully living out the life and teaching of Jesus Christ. In the world of the twenty-first century, a transforming church needs a transformed model of discipleship.

Transforming discipleship

The problem the church in the West faces is that it does not have a credible model of discipleship. 'The problem with you guys is that you don't practise your religion,' said one commentator recently to a group of North American Christian leaders. On the other hand, Muslims, Hindus and Buddhists are seen to have a credible spirituality based on the way of life widely practised by the adherents of those faiths. Gandhi recognised this problem years ago when he wrote:

If I had to face only the Sermon on the Mount, and my own interpretation of it, I should not hesitate to say, 'Oh yes, I am a Christian' . . . But negatively I can tell you that much of what passes as Christianity is a negation of the Sermon on the Mount. And please mark my words. I am not at the present moment speaking of Christian conduct. I am speaking of Christian belief. Of Christianity as it is known in the West.[1]

A rediscovery of authentic Christian discipleship will mean moving away from the privatised religion and the cheap grace that have characterised Western Christianity in the twentieth century. Being a Christian is not primarily about having a ticket to heaven as a result of 'making a commitment' to Jesus Christ. Still less is it about giving mental assent to a doctrinal statement that summarises one particular theory of the atonement. Belief in the Lord Jesus Christ is directly related to obeying Christ as Lord. Jesus himself made this perfectly clear. He said, 'Not everyone who says to me, "Lord, Lord," will enter into the kingdom of heaven, but only one who does the will of my Father in heaven' (Matthew 7:21).

James tells us that faith without works is dead. If our faith is not borne out by changed lives, there is no evidence that our faith was genuine in the first place (see James 2:14–26). Jesus said, 'If any want to become my followers, let them deny themselves and take up their cross daily and follow me' (Luke 9:23). The life of Christian discipleship is a life of self-denial. Jesus made stringent demands on all those who wanted to be his disciples. The words of Christ in the Gospels are profoundly shocking to our self-centred Western view of life. But there is little room for misunderstanding if we accept them at face value.

---

[1] Quoted in David Pytches, *Burying the Bishop* (Guildford: Eagle, 1999).

The marks of true discipleship

1. A supreme love for Jesus Christ

> Whoever comes to me and does not hate father and mother, wife and children, brothers and sisters, yes, and even life itself, cannot be my disciple. (Luke 14:26)

The word 'hate' in this passage is not intended to mean that we should hold any malice or animosity towards the members of our own family. The Jewish way of saying 'I prefer this to that' would be to say 'I like this and I hate that.' So Jesus is saying that love for our families must come second to our love for him. Jesus must come first, before all other loves. Our love for Jesus should be greater even than the love we have for those in our lives whom we love most deeply and truly.

However, the most challenging part of this saying of Jesus is probably the five words 'yes, and even life itself'. Jesus asks us to love him more than we love our own lives. He calls us, in other words, to *lay down* our lives for him. Can we bring all that life offers us, all its pleasures and joys and pursuits, and hand them over to Jesus? Some he may give back and some he may take from us. But only when everything is offered to him and made available for his will to be done, only then are we in the place he wants us to be.

2. A denial of self

> If any want to become my followers, let them deny themselves and take up their cross and follow me. (Matthew 16:24)

To deny ourselves is more than simply to practise acts of self-denial. Self-denial is usually thought of as giving up things we enjoy. In our church during Lent we are encouraged to consider making an offering to God of some voluntary acts of self-discipline or self-denial. Some people give up sweets and cake or watching television. Lent is a season of fasting and abstinence, based upon the 40 days Jesus spent fasting in the wilderness. The goal is not just to give up something, but to take specific steps to draw closer to God, above all through deepened prayer and service to others.

This kind of self-discipline is very important and has always been central to Christian spirituality. But to deny ourselves and follow Christ involves more than this. Jesus calls us to surrender our *whole will* to his lordship, to be willing to go wherever he leads us, and to do whatever he asks of us. Our way must yield to his way. We say, 'Lord, your will, not mine, be done.' This is powerfully expressed in the Covenant Service of the Methodist Church. On 25 December 1747, and on many other occasions, John Wesley strongly urged the Methodists to renew their covenant with God. His first formal Covenant Service was held in the French Church at Spitalfields on 11 August 1755. Since then the Covenant Service has been developed and revised and is widely used in Methodism and many other churches.

These words express clearly and powerfully what is meant by denying ourselves and following Christ:

THE CONGREGATION STANDS AND THE LEADER SAYS:
Beloved in Christ, let us again claim for ourselves this Covenant which God has made with us and take the yoke of Christ upon us.

To take his yoke upon us means that we are content that God appoints us to our position in life and to our work and that God be our reward.

Christ has many services to be done; some easy, others are difficult; some bring honour, others bring reproach; some are suitable to our natural inclinations and material interests, others are contrary to both. In some we may please Christ and please ourselves, in others we cannot please Christ except by denying ourselves. Yet the power to do all these things is given us in Christ, who strengthens us.

Therefore let us make this Covenant of God our own. Let us give ourselves anew to God, trusting in God's promises and relying on God's grace.

THE CONGREGATION KNEELS AND THE LEADER SAYS:

Lord God, Holy Father, since you have called us through Christ to share in this gracious Covenant, we take upon ourselves with joy the yoke of obedience, and for love of you, engage ourselves to seek and do your perfect will. We are no longer our own, but yours.

THE LEADER AND PEOPLE SAY TOGETHER:

I am no longer my own, but yours. Put me to what you will, rank me with whom you will; put me to doing, put me to suffering; let me be employed for you or laid aside for you, exalted for you or brought low for you; let me be full, let me be empty; let me have all things, let me have nothing; I freely and wholeheartedly yield all things to your pleasure and disposal. And now, glorious and blessed God, Father Son and Holy Spirit, you are mine and I am yours. So be it. And the Covenant now made on earth, let it be ratified in heaven. Amen.

3. *A deliberate choosing of the cross*

If any want to become my followers, let them deny themselves and take up their cross and follow me. (Matthew 16:24)

Sometimes we think of having a cross to bear as some kind of difficulty or problem or physical ailment we have to endure. But this is not what Jesus meant here. He spoke of those who want to be his disciples choosing a way of life marked by the cross. The cross was a symbol of shame and condemnation. It was carried by condemned prisoners on their way to a cruel and terrible execution. The cross in Jesus' time was not an attractive symbol made of silver or gold and worn on a chain around the neck!

To choose the way of the cross is consciously and deliberately to choose to live in obedience to Christ regardless of what other people think. It is to turn one's back on the ways of this world, its glamour, its rewards and its pursuits, in order to seek a better way. To live for Christ, wholeheartedly and without compromise, will lead us to being misunderstood, ridiculed and persecuted. Paul says, 'For many live as enemies of the cross of Christ . . . their god is the belly; and their glory is in their shame' (Philippians 3:18–19). William MacDonald writes:

> The cross symbolizes the shame, persecution and abuse which the world heaped upon the Son of God, and which the world will heap on all who choose to stand against the tide. Any believer can avoid the cross simply by being conformed to the world and its ways.[1]

There is a chorus we often used to sing in black congregations in South Africa:

> I have decided to follow Jesus.
> I have decided to follow Jesus.
> I have decided to follow Jesus.
> No turning back. No turning back.

---

[1] William MacDonald, *True Discipleship* (Kansas: Walterick, 1975). I am indebted to William MacDonald for the understanding of true discipleship in this section.

The cross before me, the world behind me.
The cross before me, the world behind me.
The cross before me, the world behind me.
No turning back. No turning back.

This for me sums up the way of the cross.

4. Fervent love for one another

By this everyone will know that you are my disciples, if you have love for one another. (John 13:35)

The mark of the Christian above all else is love. We can only be disciples of Jesus as part of a community. We do this together, because it is only together that we can discover the reality of what it means to have love for one another.

There are a series of one another 'sayings' in the Bible. For example:

accept one another (Romans 15:7)
love one another (John 13:34)
bear one another's burdens (Galatians 6:2)
forgive one another (Ephesians 4:32)
esteeming one another as more important (Philippians 2:3)
teach and admonish one another (Colossians 3:16)
serving one another (1 Peter 4:10)

There is great joy to be found in living our lives as part of a Christian community, which for most of us will mean being part of the community of the local church. Through good times and bad, times of rejoicing and times of mourning, in all the seasons of life, we can hold on to one another, care for one another and enable one another to continue being faithful in our walk with the Lord.

Without love for one another, Christian discipleship can become a cold, hard legalism. Christ our Lord calls and sustains us in love, mercy and grace, in our daily joys and struggles. This is not a matter of a hard taskmaster who watches our every move, waiting for us to step out of line so that he can discipline us yet again. Our Lord Jesus is the good and loving Shepherd, kind and patient with us. So we too in our life together must embody his love, generosity, patience and graciousness. If we fail to do this, we cannot in truth call ourselves 'Christian'.

5. Continuing in his word

If you continue in my word, you are truly my disciples. (John 8:31)

True discipleship is not a one-day or a one-week affair. We must persevere in his word. This is a lifetime's work. There will be times of struggle and times of weakness, even failure. Even as I write this I am very aware that I am by no means qualified to tell others about true discipleship. But my desire and the longing of my heart is to follow Christ, to know and serve him. That for me has not changed since my student days in South Africa. I have more and more come to realise that it is by grace alone that we continue in his word. Jesus sustains us through the means of grace, by his Holy Spirit, by his words and by his sacraments. He also sustains us through one another. We can only live this way of life as part of a community. The community of God's people in Jesus Christ is a precious gift, given to us by God for our mutual support, encouragement and care. This is why we should not neglect to meet together. In Hebrews 10:24 we read, 'Let us consider how to provoke one another to love and good deeds, not neglecting to meet together, as is the habit of some, but encouraging one another.'

6. Giving up our possessions

So therefore, none of you can become my disciple if you do not give up all your possessions. (Luke 14:33)

This is one of the hard sayings of Jesus. We do not often hear sermons preached on this verse. Yet this is what Jesus says to those who would be his disciples. What does this mean?

I think that what Jesus is saying here is that when we follow him our possessions are no longer ours but his. Everything belongs to him. Some are given back to us for our own use, and some are needed for the work of the kingdom.

The hard thing for many of us is taking our hands off our material wealth. We all too easily rationalise why we need this and why we should not give something else away. The key is to keep reminding ourselves that nothing belongs to us. It all belongs to the Lord and we are simply stewards. Our job is to look after and care for the property of our Master to the best of our ability. In a world of rampant materialism, where so many people, including Christians, are possessed by their possessions, this is a vitally important discipline.

We need also to be vigilant and ruthlessly honest with ourselves in deciding what we should keep and what we should give away. In a world where millions of people live in abject poverty, how can we justify spending a small fortune in African terms on luxuries like smart restaurants and expensive clothes?

When Christian mission organisations all over the world are struggling to make ends meet, we should not be preoccupied with building up surplus funds in our bank accounts, in order to provide security for the future. Jesus repeatedly warned against this. He told a parable about a man who built bigger and bigger barns to store his wealth.

> The man said to himself, 'I will say to my soul, Soul, you have ample goods laid up for many years; relax, eat, drink, be merry!' But God said to him, 'You fool! This very night your life is being demanded of you.' (Luke 12:19–20)

The challenge of true discipleship is one I face every day of my life, along with probably every other Christian who lives in the affluent Western world. But I often thank God for calling me to be ordained into the ministry of the Anglican Church. Recently I was talking to a young man who is training for the ordained ministry in Cambridge. I said to him, 'There are three reasons why it has been good for me to be ordained. First, I get to do a lot of servant ministry, like visiting the sick, whether I like it or not. Second, I am paid by the church to pray. Third, they don't pay you very much; you're never going to get rich as an Anglican priest, and I thank God very much for that.'

Obviously not everyone is called to ordination. But all disciples of Jesus are called to live simply, to pray, and to have a servant attitude to others. Even if someone is earning a large salary, the call of Jesus remains the same. We are called to live simply as servants of Jesus. In a consumer society this is not easy and we need all the help we can get to work out in practical ways what this means. In particular we need one another, to discuss, to challenge, to encourage and to pray. But the demands of true discipleship do not change for those who are affluent – they simply become more demanding.

Today what Christians call discipleship the world calls spirituality. Spirituality is strategic now. Christian spirituality is essentially a lifestyle of following Jesus. A recovery of authentic Christlike spirituality would not only transform the Western church but would powerfully impact the whole of Western society. This means something far more radical than modernising the Sunday services or the organisational structures of the church. We have to see that church is much more than something that happens in a particular building on Sundays. Church is people. Church is seven days a week. Church is relational. Church is a lifestyle of true spirituality, following Jesus into his teaching and his practices. Church is servanthood. Church is being real, especially with those who are not Christians.

This can happen anywhere. Wherever a personal encounter takes place in which Christ is present, in a sense this is church. If we have eyes to see and ears to hear we may find that there are many signs of the kingdom of God which are not in the 'church' at all but in the workplace, and on the sports fields, and out on the margins of society. Wherever Jesus is, there is church.

True discipleship therefore means living faithfully for Jesus in the real world. The church is not to be separate from the world. The purpose of the church is transformation not separation. We are to be in the world but not of the world; in the world but like Jesus. We have to ask, in a consumer society, and in a networked world, 'How do we live faithfully for Jesus?' This is about obedience but even more it is about grace. The question for many is not, 'Shall I be obedient to Christ today or not?' but 'What on earth does obedience to Christ mean in this situation at work?' and 'Am I strong enough to follow through and take the flak if I get it wrong?' It is only by the grace of God in us that this way of life is possible at all. As we work this out together, day by day, in our own locality and neighbourhood, we will be part of the future church.

3

A Changed World

The church as an agent of transformation

John Wimber was one of the most remarkable and influential church leaders of the last quarter of the twentieth century. The Vineyard movement, which arose out of his calling and vision, has become one of the fastest growing church groups in many parts of the world. John Wimber had a distinctive vision for the church. One writer, Bill Jackson, has described it as 'the quest for the radical middle ground'. Jackson sees the Vineyard as 'a movement which successfully holds in tension the great historical doctrines of the Christian faith with an ardent pursuit of the Spirit of God'. Underlying all this was the insight Wimber had about the kingdom of God.

John Wimber saw the kingdom of God as the rule or reign of God, which has broken through into human history in the person and work of Jesus Christ. For Wimber, a true understanding of the kingdom of God shows us that God is not only concerned about individuals or about the church, but about the whole of his creation. When we pray 'Your kingdom come, your will be done' we are praying that God's rule will return to the whole of the earth, and that all of his creation will come under his sovereignty and reign. The church that is kingdom-centred will be a church that believes that it is called to be God's instrument for the transformation of the whole of the earth. It will be a prophetic church that is not afraid to challenge that which is contrary to the will of God for his world.

Much of John Wimber's theology and teaching was rooted in his understanding of the kingdom. For example, his teaching on healing starts from the perspective of the kingdom, and healing is therefore seen as overall and inclusive, rather than 'specific healings'. For Wimber healing is wholeness of the total person and his or her environment. Wimber writes:

> Keep in mind that healing is often the same Greek word, *sozo*, which is also translated salvation, and basically means 'saved out from under the devil's power and restored into the wholeness of God's order and well-being by the power of God's Spirit,' e.g. the ten lepers were healed and cleansed in Luke 17:14–17, and Jesus says their faith saved them (v.19). Healing (salvation) is used not only in regard to physical or spiritual wholeness, but also for every other aspect of human life and environment that is in any way under the power or influence of the devil (Luke 4:18). Healings, in this all-inclusive sense, are signs of the presence and power of God's kingdom (Luke 7:19–22).[1]

I too have increasingly come to see how important the kingdom of God is in the Bible. It is one of the central themes in the teaching of Jesus. It is interesting to note that

---

[1] John Wimber, *Healing Seminar* (Anaheim: Mercy Publishing, 1987).

Jesus said very little about the church but he said a great deal about the kingdom. This does not mean that the church was not important to Jesus. But it seems that when the church has its focus on the kingdom of God, then the church will grow and be healthy. However, when the church is preoccupied with the business of the church, then it becomes inward looking and less and less effective.

The kingdom of God means literally the rule or reign of God. Whenever we see the rule or reign of God extended and God's will being done in the lives of people and in his world, then we are seeing his kingdom come. So the work of the kingdom is the work of transformation.

Jesus came proclaiming in word and deed the good news of the kingdom. That meant that people's lives were transformed as they received the good news of Jesus. It also meant that God's purpose in Christ was to redeem and make whole every aspect of human life and the environment, indeed all of creation.

When Jesus began his public ministry he gave a brief summary of his whole purpose and mission:

> Now after John was arrested, Jesus came to Galilee, proclaiming the good news of God, and saying, 'The time is fulfilled, and the kingdom of God has come near; repent, and believe in the good news.' (Mark 1:14–15)

Jesus not only spoke and taught a great deal about the kingdom of God. He also did many mighty works and miracles, which can be seen as signs of the kingdom. So in the coming of Jesus the kingdom of God broke through into human history with extraordinary transforming power, to confront and overcome sin, sickness, death, injustice, and all the powers of the evil one.

The primary miracle that marks the presence and power

of the kingdom of God in and through Jesus is changed lives. Jesus called people to turn away from sin, from all that was wrong and unrighteous in their lives, and to believe in him and follow him. The result of this is a changed heart and changed lives, in the power of Jesus. Jesus is the specialist in heart transplants. He fulfils the words of Ezekiel 36:26: 'A new heart I will give you, and a new spirit I will put within you; and I will remove from your body the heart of stone and give you a heart of flesh.'

I have seen the reality of the life-changing power of Jesus over and over again, in my own life, in the lives of many of my friends, and in the lives of many people whom I have had the privilege of knowing through my ministry in the church. To see a person turn to Christ and experience the new life he brings through the power of the Holy Spirit is one of the most amazing miracles one can ever encounter. And I have seen this happen again and again. Jesus is able to transform any human life and any human heart. Nothing is impossible for him. There is no one who cannot turn to Jesus and be changed. Paul of Tarsus, Francis of Assisi, John Newton, C. S. Lewis, Stephen Lungu, Chuck Colson – the list goes on and on. For 2,000 years, men and women in countless different civilisations and cultures have discovered the reality of this truth, as St Paul himself did: 'So if anyone is in Christ, there is a new creation: everything old has passed away; see, everything has become new!' (2 Corinthians 5:17).

In our church, Colin Bowman is a young man who has within the last year become a Christian. I asked him to describe in his own words what has happened to him.

Ian   Colin, can you tell me how long you've been a
       Christian?

Colin   Well, I said the prayer of commitment just before Christmas, so it's been just over ten months now.

Ian   Why did you start coming to All Saints Church?

Colin   I was interested in the Christian faith before I actually became a Christian. Then Andrew Woodman, who knows my brother Ross, wondered if I would like to come along to the coffee bar which he was running at All Saints. And having been to the coffee bar for a few weeks I decided that there was no harm in my actually going to a church service. I hadn't been to a church service for years. Gradually over the weeks after that my interest just peaked in different things about the Christian faith. Obviously there was a lot of self-doubt within me. Is this true? Is this right for me? But then very gradually all these questions were answered in little ways that only I would know about. In the end I came to a point where I thought, 'Yes, this is for me actually.'

Ian   So what actually led you to make the decision to become a Christian yourself?

Colin   It was the realisation that all the different aspects of the Christian faith related to me personally, like reading the Bible for a while and understanding that this was written 2,000 years ago and it still has the same relevance now as it did 2,000 years ago. I would say that I always had a problem thinking about God as some supernatural being who is out there, and I had nothing in common with him. But reading the Bible I could see that this applies to my life, it applies to my friends' lives, it applies to everybody's lives. That gradually led me to find God.

Ian   So you actually became a Christian during a service

at All Saints Church. Can you tell me how that happened?

Colin   Yes. It was the story of doubting Thomas. Thomas doubted whether the disciples had actually seen Jesus. Jesus came back and said, 'Put your fingers in my wounds, and in my side, and touch me. I am here and I have risen again.' It was these kinds of doubts that applied to me. It was, 'How do I know you're really there? I can't feel you. I can't touch you. I can't literally have a human conversation with you.' I had a long chat with Anne and Craig and they said, 'The only way that you're going to find out is to let God come and speak to you.' And all three of us prayed a prayer of commitment. It was a wonderful experience. I felt my heart beat a little bit faster, and my feet felt very solid, just where they were, and I felt that I really couldn't move. And after the prayer the others said that they could see it in my face, and my reactions, and my breathing. They could see that God had come down and he showed me exactly what he wanted to show me. I came to a point where I said, 'I must see to believe,' and I said the prayer and in my own way I felt what I wanted to feel. I wanted to feel God's presence within me, and that's exactly what he did.

Ian   So since then you have grown a lot in your faith. What part has being in the church here and being with other Christians played in this for you?

Colin   Being with other Christians there are things that I can talk about, things where the church has helped me to grow. It's like being in a family.

Ian   What has helped you to move on in your faith since you prayed that prayer of commitment?

Colin   Reading the Bible. That has to be the start. And being with people who have been Christians for a bit longer and listening to their experiences. Being able to talk over any problems that I may have with people my own age. For someone like myself who is 21, who has just come into a Christian faith, the stereotypical Christian for a non-Christian is a more elderly person who goes to church on Sunday and who doesn't have anything to do with the community. But being a younger person and being able to talk over any problems with someone of the same age is a wonderful experience.

Ian   Then there has been a very big change in your life, hasn't there?

Colin   Yes, there has. I have this wristband which says WWJD. There are certain situations where I can just look at it and it just quickly flicks 'What would Jesus do in this situation?' He wouldn't get angry. He wouldn't get violent. He wouldn't start judging people. So just looking at four letters makes you test that back. It reflects on everybody else too, because once they see you doing that they think, 'That's not right for me to judge. That's not right for me to get angry.' They are looking at God through you because they know you're a Christian. They know that God has worked within you, which means that there's nothing stopping him from working within them. They are the sort of people who know the person I was before and the sort of problems I've been through. It helps other people to change their stereotypes of Christians.

The gospel, or good news, of the kingdom of God is a message of transformation. The purpose of the transforming church is to pray and work for the extension of the kingdom. The spearhead of this purpose or mission is evangelism. Evangelism is the task of bringing people to a personal knowledge and experience of the saving and transforming power of Jesus. Without changed lives we cannot see transformed churches, or communities, or nations. Without a new heart, and without the indwelling of the Holy Spirit, human endeavour cannot reveal and bring into reality the life, character and purposes of Jesus and the kingdom of God. The world will not be changed unless we begin with evangelism.

However, the work of the church is not to be confined to personal salvation and a privatised faith that does not connect with the wider issues of society. That is not the intention of the gospel as we see it in the life and teaching of Jesus. John Wimber describes a whole range of ways in which we experience the reality of the kingdom of God in and through Jesus Christ. These include

(a) deliverance from demonic power and influence
(b) forgiveness of sin
(c) life and resurrection from death
(d) sharing God's abundance with the oppressed poor
(e) growing in the community of the kingdom
(f) reigning in life through Christ[1]

These are the realities of living in the kingdom of God, which means living under the rule and reign of God. The task and mission of the church is to make these realities

---

[1] John Wimber, *Healing Seminar* (Anaheim: Mercy Publishing, 1987).

known in word and deed. If we do this, we can be an agent of transformation at every level of human life and society.

A new model of mission

In a world which is seeking for an authentic spirituality, God's church must attempt to present the gospel of Jesus Christ in creative and imaginative ways. We must not allow our structures to get in the way; rather they must serve the gospel. And if this means reshaping then we must have the courage to do so.[1]

In November 1999 a major citywide mission was held in Cambridge in England. Around 50 churches participated in this mission, which was the culmination of two years of prayer, planning and preparation. The total budget was in the region of £35,000. During the mission week itself, a large team of missioners came from all around the United Kingdom to work with local Christians in proclaiming the gospel of Jesus Christ.

The impact and effectiveness of the mission was difficult to assess accurately. Certainly a few people made commitments of faith in Christ, while others filled in response cards at the various meetings. Yet the mission was for many people, even in the participating churches, a disappointing and frustrating experience. For me the Cambridge '@2000' mission (in November 1999) raised serious questions about the models of mission that churches in Britain should be using as we begin the twenty-first century. Clearly the model that worked well in the 1950s and 1960s needs to be rethought. We can no longer think about mission simply in terms of

---

[1] Bishop Rubin Philip, after his election to be the ninth Anglican Bishop of Natal, South Africa, on 21 September 1999.

holding a series of evangelistic meetings with a gifted preacher or speaker presenting a challenge to those attending to receive Jesus Christ as their personal Saviour. This approach does not seem to work in a city like Cambridge at the end of the twentieth century.

I was heavily involved in the planning and preparation for the @2000 mission. I speak as someone who saw the mission unfold 'from the inside'. The mission initially seemed to me to be the right initiative for the churches of Cambridge at the beginning of the new millennium. But perhaps it should also be seen as the last of an old, outdated style of mission, which is now giving way to a new vision for the church in Britain, and in many other parts of our global postmodern society.

Salt and light

In the Sermon on the Mount, Jesus gave two pictures of how Christians could and should bring change to their world. He said:

> You are the salt of the earth. But if the salt loses its saltiness, how can it be made salty again? It is no longer good for anything, except to be thrown out and trampled . . . You are the light of the world. A city on a hill cannot be hidden. Neither do people light a lamp and put it under a bowl. Instead they put it on its stand, and it gives light to everyone in the house. (Matthew 5:13–15 NIV)

A new vision for the church and its mission will involve rediscovering what it means to be salt and light. The purpose of the church is to bring about change in the name of Jesus. It is to be the salt that brings out the taste and gives distinctiveness to something that would otherwise be bland and pointless. Salt preserves; it cannot be overlooked, because its very nature is to pervade the whole, to bring out its true flavour.

When I was at boarding school in South Africa, I often went back to school at the beginning of term with a few sticks of biltong in my bag. Biltong is dried raw meat, preserved with salt, and is delicious to those brought up on it. On our farm I can remember watching my father cutting strips of beef (or occasionally springbok), and I would help him salt the meat before we hung it up to dry out. Because of the salt the meat did not go rotten. Rather, it matured, over time, to become a true South African delicacy.

Biltong originated hundreds of years ago when the Voortrekkers (Afrikaner pioneers) used this method to preserve meat in their ox-wagons, as they trekked vast distances into the Southern African interior. Salt makes a huge difference to raw meat. Without salt it would quickly decay and make anyone who ate it sick.

It is the nature of light to drive out darkness. When a powerful torch is switched on in a dark place, the darkness has no option but to flee. Light is also an agent of change. The entrance of light dramatically changes a situation such as a darkened room. When light is present, people can see where they are going. Light banishes the fear of bumping into obstacles, or of dangers hiding in the darkness. Light exposes the reality around us, and enables us to see things as they really are.

Salt and light provide key images for us to understand the way in which Jesus intends his disciples to engage with the world. But what does this mean for the church at the beginning of the twenty-first century? If salt and light are the key images in shaping a redefined vision of the church, what does this mean in practical terms?

African Enterprise is an organisation working in many

African countries, from South Africa to Egypt and Ethiopia. Its aim is to 'evangelise the cities of Africa through word and deed in partnership with the church'. Recently African Enterprise has been rethinking and reformulating its strategy in order to move to a model of mission relevant to the twenty-first century. Songe Chibambo of the African Enterprise team in South Africa described their vision for future missions in these words:

> AE's purpose in South Africa is to help build the Kingdom of God by calling together and enabling the church to be a transforming, evangelistic presence in the city and the nation. Therefore a mission will be a process of empowerment and not an event.

This sums up the new vision of mission emerging in many parts of the world. Mission in the twenty-first century is about

- the kingdom of God
- the church, and especially the local church
- transformation and evangelism inextricably linked together
- a vision for the local community, the city and the nation
- a process of empowerment rather than an event
- a commitment to building relationships among church leaders

As the churches in a town or city grasp the vision, a process of transformation will take hold. Its impact will lead to evangelistic effectiveness and church growth, and also a change for the better in many aspects of community life, such as crime, drug abuse, education and so on. This is the 'salt and light' effect of the kingdom of God. This is the transforming church in action.

Transformed nations

The nation of South Africa provides us in our time with one of the most compelling and extraordinary stories of God's transforming power in the life of a nation. South Africa at the beginning of the twenty-first century still faces many challenges and problems, most notably poverty, AIDS, unemployment and crime. But it is also a nation that has been extraordinarily transformed, even within the last ten years. How did this happen? Clearly there are different possible explanations. But many who lived in South Africa through the years of transition to democracy will tell you that it was the hand of God that brought the nation through its darkest moments. And there were moments of desperate crisis, when the future of the nation hung in the balance.

I shall never forget the time of the assassination of Chris Hani, or the Boipatong massacre, or the final breakdown of negotiations to prepare the way for an inclusive election, with only a matter of weeks to go. We were in a critical situation and apprehension filled many people's hearts as the day of the election drew closer. I wrote in my diary on 2 April 1994, 'I pray that you will bring this nation safely through the next five weeks, O Lord, in Jesus Christ our Lord.'

On Sunday 17 April 1994 I went with a group from our church to the Jesus Peace Rally at Kings Park rugby stadium in Durban. We joined some 30,000 people who gathered before God in united prayer and repentance, crying to him to save our land. We remembered the verse in 2 Chronicles 7:14, which says:

> . . . if my people who are called by my name humble themselves, pray, seek my face, and turn from their wicked ways, then I will hear from heaven, and will forgive their sin and heal their land.

We cried to God to intervene, even at this late hour, to forgive and to be merciful to our beloved country, South Africa.

What we did not know was that even as we were praying an amazing chain of events was taking place. Washington Okumu, a Kenyan Christian diplomat, was flying to Cape Town that very afternoon to meet with Nelson Mandela. Washington Okumu had been asked by Michael Cassidy to come to South Africa some months previously in order to work behind the scenes as a mediator and bridge builder with the key political figures. As the tension escalated, a final attempt was made to reach a negotiated settlement, with Henry Kissinger and Lord Carrington acting as the key mediators. These talks had broken down and civil war seemed inevitable. South Africa was heading directly for the bloodbath so many people had predicted.

But then, God did an extraordinary thing. On Tuesday 19 April, two days after the Jesus Peace Rally, an inclusive settlement was announced at the Union Buildings in Pretoria, and this led directly to the peaceful and historic elections the following week. In order for this settlement to be implemented, parliament was recalled to meet on the day before the election. Eighty million ballot papers were adapted in the days immediately prior to the elections by placing specially printed stickers on the already printed ballot papers.

The elections took place from 27 to 28 April 1994, and they led directly to the formation of a new non-racial government under the new president, Nelson Mandela.

How did this happen? There is no doubt in my mind that this was a miracle. *The Citizen* is the main daily morning newspaper in Johannesburg. On Wednesday 20 April their editorial comment was headlined 'MIRACLE'. They said:

Not in our wildest dreams could we have expected such an eleventh hour compromise. We have said on several occasions that only a miracle could save the election from being held amidst mounting conflict – and that miracle is at hand.

On 21 April 1994 Washington Okumu was interviewed on the BBC World Service. He was asked about the Jesus Peace Rally in Durban, and the role of prayer in the inclusive settlement. He said, 'I believe in the power of prayer. It is amazing that [this happened] at the time that prayer was going on. How can you say that is a coincidence? That is definitely God's miracle.'

The result of what happened in those amazing weeks was the transformation of South Africa. I was there. I stood in the queues, waiting to cast my vote, together with millions of my fellow South Africans of all races and backgrounds. I now know that miracles do happen in the history of nations. I know too that the church and Christian people can become the agent of transformation not just of individual lives and communities but of nations. We, the people of God, can be his instrument in the transformation of our world. For this to happen we shall need to be fully involved in the affairs and the needs of our world, at every level. We must be ready to seize every opportunity to be counted for Christ and to make a difference in his name. We shall be called upon to work ceaselessly for justice and for reconciliation, and to oppose the forces of evil and violence and hatred, as did many South African Christians over many long years during the time of apartheid.

Jesus has called his church to change the world. It was said of the early Christians that they turned the world upside down. We are the instruments of his peace. We work and pray, day and night, for the coming of the kingdom of God, which is the rule and reign of God in all of the world. Jesus said, 'To what should I compare the kingdom of God? It is like yeast that a woman took and mixed in with three measures of flour until all of it was leavened' (Luke 13:20–21).

PART 2

The Church that Builds Relationships

I give you a new commandment, that you love one another.
Just as I have loved you, you also should love one another.

(John 13:34)

4

The People-Centred Church

The transforming church is a church where people matter.
Good relationships are essential to the growth and health of
the body of Christ. There is no other way for the church to
grow and to be healthy except through people working
together and sharing their lives under the headship of Jesus.

> But speaking the truth in love, we must grow up in every way
> into him who is the head, into Christ, from whom the whole
> body, joined and knitted together by every ligament with which
> it is equipped, as each part is working properly, promotes the
> body's growth in building itself up in love. (Ephesians 4:15–16)

That is Paul's vision and the New Testament understanding of the church. Paul speaks of the church as the body of
Christ, with each part working together and building itself
up in love. But what does this mean in practice?

I have now had over 20 years' experience of ministry and
leadership in the church, on two continents, and in very
different communities. All my experience of church leadership and ministry tells me that healthy churches are churches
where people really matter and feel that they belong.

I have seen many models of leadership in local churches. Some work, and some, frankly, don't. The kinds of leadership that fail to produce growth and health in the church are those that do not take the people of God seriously. If pastors or leaders have a vision, they must be willing to take the time to enable others to buy into that vision. It doesn't matter how much they believe in the vision, or even whether it's the right or the wrong vision; none of this will count for much if the pastor does not have the trust and confidence of the people and take them on the journey.

It takes time to win trust. It takes time to care, to listen and to serve. No leaders in any organisation will fully realise their goals and plans unless they are willing to give time to those they depend upon for the fulfilment of the vision.

There are no short cuts to winning trust and respect. It is not enough to say, 'Trust me. I've prayed about this, and I know that this is what God is saying to this church.' Unless we respect our people enough to share our vision with them, on the basis of a relationship of trust, we cannot expect them to give their full backing and commitment to what, after all, is our vision not theirs. The vision has to become a shared vision, which will mean that it has to grow and change along the way. This all takes time and involves risk, but it is a direct consequence of taking people seriously. I believe that there is no other way to be an effective church leader.

Another way of saying this is that it's all about working as a team. Shared ministry is about team building. Leaders who want to enable shared ministry have to be team players and team builders. I am committed to team building in the church I lead. I know of no other way to grow and equip the church for mission and ministry. Team building is a strategy, and it is also a costly and time-consuming process. It is a model of ministry I have deliberately chosen, chiefly because I see it as the New Testament model for the church. It stands in direct contrast to the old 'one-man-band' model of ordained ministry. I have consistently aimed to develop and to sharpen my own skills in this model of leadership, by learning both from other church leaders who are effective in team building, and from the best models in secular management and leadership. Delegation, for example, is a key skill, and it is not as easy as some may think. If we fail to delegate we fail to empower and release people to use their gifts fully, because there is someone else doing the job.

No leader can truthfully claim to 'get it right' all the time. As leaders, we are continually learning and growing, and those whom we have the privilege of leading are our teachers. We learn from them, and they learn from us, and the Holy Spirit is the one who directs and teaches us all to make us more like Jesus. That is the Jesus way of being church together.

Transforming leadership

Transforming leadership seeks transformation in the church and in the world. It is also leadership that is willing to be transformed. So transformation in the church and its leaders is a process, which is never finished. God by his Spirit is continuously transforming us from one degree of glory to another (2 Corinthians 3:18).

I see five key commitments that make up a transforming model of leadership. This model of leadership needs the following commitments on the part of the leader:

1. A commitment to personal transformation.
2. A commitment to servant leadership.

3. A commitment to the gifts and power of the Holy Spirit.
4. A commitment to shared leadership.
5. A commitment to enabling others.

1. A commitment to personal transformation

Personal transformation is the result of a daily working together with the Spirit of God in order that we may become more and more like Jesus. This is rooted in a daily time alone with God. No Christian leaders can hope to be effective or fruitful in serving Christ unless they are spending time with God. The work of Christ is not accomplished through human effort and resources. It is the work of the Holy Spirit through obedient and faithful men and women. We cannot be obedient unless we first take time to listen to God, and to hear from him what his will and purposes are, for us and for the church.

The result of prayer and obedience will also be transformation. A leader who is constantly learning and growing will lead a church that also is a learning, growing community of believers.

Transformation begins ultimately with God, but it also begins with leaders. A transforming church needs leaders who are being transformed themselves, under the hand of God. The letter of the Hebrews tells us that 'the Lord disciplines those whom he loves, and chastises every child whom he accepts' (Hebrews 12:6).

We can co-operate with the disciplines of the Lord, or we can be stubborn and unyielding, so that the Lord has to refine and chastise us in ways that are sometimes painful and hard. It is far better to learn quickly the ways of the Lord, and where necessary to be willing to change our habits and our preferences, so that we may know the peace and blessing of God.

Leaders open to transformation are those who are willing to listen to God, and willing to learn from God and from other leaders, and who are not just stuck in a particular way of doing things.

For me this has meant paying careful attention to the matter of priorities. I have come to understand that prayer is the priority of my life. Prayer informs and orders all the other concerns and demands I face from day to day. Through prayer and times of retreat I am helped to discern the difference between the urgent and the truly important. I know that all the work of the church is important, but some things are more important for me to do than others. Some things should be left to other people, while there are some things that only I can do. There are visits that can be made by a member of our pastoral team, and there are visits that I as the rector need to make. I need to hear daily the promptings of the Holy Spirit. By spending time in quietness and reflection before God, I am able to reflect upon my life, and to discern God's priorities for me. This includes knowing how much time I should give to work, and how much I should give to my family, to friends, and to caring for my own health through exercise and sport and relaxation.

I aim to live a balanced and healthy life, in every dimension of my life, in order that I may glorify God and serve him to the best of my ability. By doing this I also hope to model and encourage a proper balance and wholeness in the other leaders who work with me. I do not want my fellow leaders to be burnt out or overworked, but I do want them to have time for God, and for their families, and for themselves. In my experience all of this flows out of the centrality of prayer. When we put first things first it is amazing to see how other things fall into their proper place.

2. A commitment to servant leadership

Christian leadership is not about status seeking. Jesus set an example of servant leadership, in particular when he washed his disciples' feet and said, 'I have set you an example, that you also should do as I have done to you' (John 13:15). Jesus is the man for others. He explicitly calls his disciples, and especially those who would be leaders, to be servants of all: 'whoever wishes to become great among you must be your servant, and whoever wishes to be first among you must be slave of all' (Mark 10:43–44).

I am sometimes tempted to think that I am too busy to spend time with some of the apparently less important groups in our church. I know that I need to be present when decisions are being made that affect the future of the church. But do I need to visit the local sheltered housing complex to take Holy Communion to a small group of elderly people? Is it important for me to visit old Edgar, who before the war used to be shepherd on a farm south of Cambridge, and who is now 85 and has recurring chest problems? Or should I delegate that to someone else? The words of Jesus tell me that no leader should ever be too busy or too important to have time for seemingly 'unimportant' people, because such people are extremely important to Jesus. When we cease to have time for the weak, the poor and the 'insignificant', then we cease to be fit to be called Christian leaders.

The leaders God seems to be using in building unity and transformation seem to me to be servant leaders, leaders who have a love for the people and a love for the church – not just their own church, but the whole church of the Lord Jesus. We should never forget that God loves the church, with its good points and bad, strengths and weaknesses. The church is the bride of Christ and it is the body of Christ. The

Lord loves the church, and leaders who are close to the heart of God will love the church too.

3. A commitment to the gifts and power of the Holy Spirit

Last year I received a Christmas letter from a friend who is the rector of a church in South Africa. He wrote:

> The parish has experienced amazing growth in these past two years, and in order to accommodate the additional people coming to worship, we have now started a third Sunday service in the evening. There is a freedom in our worship, which is wonderful to experience, as we rely on the blessing, empowerment and manifestation of the gifts of the Holy Spirit.

Growing churches are often in my experience those churches willing to actively seek and be open to the gifts and empowering of the Holy Spirit. Only the Holy Spirit can bring life to the church. We need to pray, again and again, 'Come Holy Spirit. Come and revive us. Come and breathe new life into your church.' Having prayed this prayer, we need to give space for the Spirit to move in our worship and our services. Sometimes our services leave little room for God to do all he wants to do.

In our Sunday evening worship, after the time of teaching, we allow time for the Holy Spirit to impart into our lives what we have heard being taught from the Bible. This may involve standing and waiting in God's presence, with the use of words of prophecy, wisdom and knowledge (1 Corinthians 12:6–11). There may also be prayer for healing, and for other needs, with anointing with oil and the laying on of hands (James 5:14). Many people will simply remain for some time in an attitude of worship before God and openness to the Holy Spirit. We rely on the presence and gifts of the Holy Spirit to change our lives and to enable us to live out the gospel.

Leaders who are being used by God to bring about changed lives and community transformation are leaders who are personally and publicly open to the gifts of the Holy Spirit. It is only by the Spirit of God that the miracle of transformation in Christ can take place. As we cry out with all our hearts to the Lord and ask him to send his Spirit upon us, we find that, again and again, the Lord is good and merciful, and he sends his Holy Spirit upon his people. The Holy Spirit is sometimes a disturber of the peace and quiet in our churches. He comes both to comfort and to make us uncomfortable. But the church desperately needs the empowering of the Holy Spirit. Paul knew this in his own life and ministry. He wrote:

> And I came to you in weakness and in fear and in much trembling. My speech and my proclamation were not with plausible words of wisdom, but with a demonstration of the Spirit and of power, so that your faith might rest not on human wisdom but on the power of God. (1 Corinthians 2:3–5)

4. A commitment to shared leadership

It is vital to note that local church leadership in the New Testament was always shared. I have throughout my ministry shared my leadership with others, lay and ordained, male and female, in whom I have recognised a gift or ministry of leadership in our local church. At times we have called this leadership group the 'elders', or 'the ministry team', or 'the leadership team'. As the rector, I act as the presiding elder, because in the church canons I carry the ultimate responsibility for the pastoral oversight of our church. I am accountable, as a man under authority, to the bishop under whom I serve. But I also seek to be accountable to the other leaders in the church, and to share all key decisions and policy with them.

Shared leadership can take a variety of forms. In my own experience I have worked both with an eldership and a staff team, as well as taking seriously the legal and canonical role of the churchwardens and PCC (Parochial Church Council). However, I have found particular value in working with an eldership or ministry team, where we meet, usually every month, to pray together and to seek God's will for our church. Here we are able, as leaders, to listen together to what the Lord is saying, and to discern together what may or may not be his word to us. We need to be accountable to one another both for our personal lives and for the exercise of our gifts and ministries in the church. We also commit ourselves to pray and intercede for the church, and for one another. From this shared leadership has flowed many of the most significant and fruitful initiatives that I have seen in my ministry. Indeed this has not been *my* ministry; it has been a shared ministry, shared with others, and shared with the Lord.

Andrew Kirk, quoted by David Watson in *I Believe in the Church*, suggests six principles of Christian ministry.[1]

1. No distinction either in form, language or theory between clergy and laity was ever accepted by the New Testament church.
2. The ministry is co-extensive with the entire church (1 Corinthians 12:7).
3. The local church in the apostolic age always functioned under a plurality of leadership.
4. There are no uniform models for ministry in the New Testament; the patterns are flexible and versatile.

---

[1] David Watson, *I Believe in the Church* (London: Hodder & Stoughton, 1978).

5. In the New Testament church can be found both leadership and authority, but no kind of hierarchical structure.
6. There is one, and only one, valid distinction which the New Testament appears to recognise within the ministry, apart from the different functions to which we have been alluding: the distinction between *local* and *itinerant* ministries.

These principles are immensely important. Flexibility of structures and a plurality of leadership are vital for healthy church growth and development. It is important also to recognise that both men and women may be called and gifted by God for ministry and leadership. Gender roles in our society and culture have changed enormously over the past generation. A transforming church will recognise that many women are gifted by God to be leaders, and this will be reflected in the plurality of leadership.

5. A commitment to enabling others

Participation   Someone who has recently joined our church said to me, 'What I find so attractive here is the active participation of so many people.' A healthy church is one that makes room for every member of the body to exercise a particular gift or ministry. There are many ways to enable this to happen. It does take careful planning, and rosters are a wonderful aid to enabling people to become more involved. Our church, like many others, has rosters for everything from making tea and coffee, to preaching and leading services, to cleaning the church and tidying the pews. The person (or persons) who draws up these rosters performs a vital role in the life of the church.

Just as important, however, is a willingness in the church membership and leadership to allow new people to take on tasks and ministries. I am always looking for new people to encourage and find a role for in the church. This means that things keep on being done differently, and that we must allow people room to learn and sometimes to make mistakes. There is a risk involved in opening up the church in this way. The first time someone preaches, or leads the worship, or prays for healing is always a time where faith has to be present, both for the congregation and for the person involved! It's not always perfect first time! We are all human, and the church needs to be human too. There is a danger in trying to be too professional, too polished. We aim to offer our best to God, but we aim also to be gentle and patient, with ourselves and with one another. It is important to remember that in the church we are not aiming for perfection; we simply want to bring an offering to God, and give him the best we can.

Discernment   In enabling people to exercise a wider range of gifts and ministries, leaders themselves need the gift of discernment. In his first letter to Timothy, Paul says, 'Do not be hasty in the laying on of hands' (1 Timothy 5:22 NIV). Leaders in the church need great wisdom in all their dealings with the people of God. James says, 'If any of you lacks wisdom, let him ask God, who gives to all generously and without reproaching, and it will be given to him' (James 1:5 RSV). As a leader I am constantly trying to discern what God is doing by his Spirit in the church. I then seek to bless and encourage what I see God doing.

Discernment in sensitive matters of church life is greatly helped when such decisions are made in the context of shared leadership. Sometimes we may be able to share such issues with only one or two co-leaders, on the basis of strict confidentiality. But I try never to make a decision that affects the direction of the church or the life or lives of individual members without a shared discernment of what seems to be the right way forward in the sight of God. Of course this means that all true discernment is rooted in prayer.

Feedback and encouragement Shared leadership and shared ministry thrives on positive feedback. Just as children and teenagers need encouragement and affirmation, so do all those who give of themselves in the life and ministry of the church. I try always to give feedback to anyone who either preaches or leads worship in our church. If there is something that needs to be said, it is my responsibility as Rector to do that.

This in itself is a pastoral task that requires wisdom and sensitivity. I personally do not find it easy to cope with highly critical comments about my sermon as I talk to people at the church door after the service! The right time and place has to be found, and the right words and tone as well. Most people need a good measure of encouragement and affirmation, and will grow and develop their gifts in a positive and supportive environment. Criticism and rebuke has to be administered carefully and wisely, but there are times when it has to be done.

I also try to thank people personally for whatever they have done in the life of the church. It makes a huge difference to know that you are appreciated. What is done in the church is done primarily for the Lord. But if the pastor or rector has noticed and has said something positive, for most people that certainly does make a difference.

Small groups

My experience has convinced me that small groups are the key to the development of shared ministry and a people-centred church. It is in a small group that we discover our own gifts and the gifts of one another, all of which are vitally important for the health and growth of the church.

Paul says:

> Indeed, the body does not consist of one member but of many. If the foot were to say, 'Because I am not a hand, I do not belong to the body', that would not make it any less a part of the body . . . As it is, there are many members, yet one body. The eye cannot say to the hand, 'I have no need of you', nor again the head to the feet, 'I have no need of you.' (1 Corinthians 12:14–15, 20–21)

It is in the small group that the meaning of this is really worked out in practice. It is in the small group that we learn to be the servants of Christ to one another. It is here that we can know one another's needs, wash one another's feet, and care effectively for one another, as Jesus expected of his disciples. The small group is the key to discipleship and ministry in the local congregation. Juan Carlos Ortiz, the Argentinean pastor and writer, describes in one of his books how, as he looked at his church in Argentina, he came to realise that his church was centred on *membership* rather than on *discipleship*.[1]

The duties of church membership are listed in our church as follows:

- To follow the example of Christ in home and daily life and to bear witness to him.
- To be regular in private prayer day by day.
- To read the Bible carefully.
- To come to church every Sunday.

---

[1] Juan Carlos Ortiz, *Disciple* (London: Lakeland, 1975).

- To receive the Holy Communion faithfully and regularly.
- To give personal service to church, neighbours and community.
- To uphold the standard of marriage entrusted by Christ to his church.
- To care that children are brought up to love and serve the Lord.
- To give money for the work of the parish and diocese and for the work of the church at home and overseas.

If you do these things you are normally regarded as a good member of the church. But Ortiz says that he came to realise that this is like being a member of a club. You attend the club, pay the monthly membership fees, and abide by the rules. That is what club members do. But Jesus did not talk about membership; he talked about discipleship. And the New Testament doesn't talk about a club. It speaks about a body or a family. In the New Testament the church is the body of Christ, and every member is a disciple. Ortiz says that he had a club type of congregation. The church needed to be transformed from a club to a family. So he took a group of members from the church and formed a cell group in his home, and started to share his life with them to make disciples of them. He opened his home to them. They ate together and went out into the country together. They came to sleep in his home; he went to sleep in their homes. Through the sharing of their lives they became a family. In due course they each took other members of the church and did the same thing with them. Eventually after three years the whole membership of the church had been drawn into these small groups, and the church had become a family. The whole structure of the church had been transformed. This involved some radical decisions. For example, for one whole month they held no services in their church building. They only met in homes, and on Sundays went to visit Roman Catholic and Baptist churches and other congregations in the local area.

The importance of this is that a church that is a *family* is not dependent upon a building. It can meet anywhere – in homes, in a school hall, on the beach, anywhere. Also, such a church is not totally dependent upon the minister or the pastor for its ongoing life and ministry. In a church like this the work of ministry is the responsibility of the whole body. Ministry is taking place all the time, every time a group meets, or even when two disciples meet and pray together or care for one another in some way.

All over the world churches are rediscovering the value of the small group. Of course this is nothing new. Jesus chose a group of twelve disciples with whom he shared his life fully. He taught them, worked with them and then sent them out two by two to put into practice what they had learnt. John Wesley founded what became the Methodist Church on what he called the class meeting. He made sure that converts were quickly fed into small groups in which they were grounded in Christian living by the open sharing of their lives with one another. In South America there has been a tremendous growth in what are called basic Christian communities, where there is a deep level of caring for one another and sharing of resources, rooted in a common life of prayer and worship.

So the possibilities these groups offer to the church are exciting and significant. But there are some important things we must take into account if such groups are to function effectively:

1. Leadership is vital to the success of the groups. Group leaders need to be trained, and to receive ongoing support

and training. We have found that it is necessary to make this a priority if our small groups are to grow and be successful. This means regular meetings of group leaders, and close personal contact between the group leaders and the pastor or church leader.

2. Healthy groups grow and multiply. This means that the groups should not become too big. Twelve has been found to be the maximum number for a small group to function effectively without some members tending to be left out. Ideally a group should number between a minimum of five and a maximum of twelve people. The groups should be undergirded by a commitment to grow and split as soon as they reach a certain size.

3. Commitment to the group is necessary from all the members. Relationships within groups can only be built up if the group members are prepared to commit themselves to consistent attendance and participation in meetings. However, we are aware that in many of our groups there are members whose work and travel mean that they are not able to attend the group on a regular basis. They none the less want to be part of the group. We have learnt to make allowance for this, and to encourage such people to consider themselves as part of the group even when they are away from home, and to participate as much as they are able.

4. A group should meet at whatever time is most suitable for its members, whether that be in the morning, the afternoon or the evening. Ortiz says that some of his groups met at 6 am because the men worked at night. Some even met at 2 am.

5. The purpose is making disciples. As Ortiz points out, the object of discipleship is not just the information of the mind but the *formation of life*. As someone has said, 'When all is said and done, too much is said and too little is done.' This is particularly true of many small groups. Faith in Christ entails a life of *obedience*. In a small group we aim to discover and to put into practice what this means for each individual Christian.

The groups should be involved in studying the Bible, not simply as an intellectual exercise, but rather as the basis for faith-sharing. In this, the Bible is applied to the realities of daily life, and leads to discussion and sharing about our own lives and our experience of God at work. Faith-sharing aims to help the group members to apply their Christian faith to all the circumstances and challenges of their life, at work, at home, in their private worlds, and so on. Faith-sharing also enables them to gain the confidence to speak openly about their faith to others.

The intention of the groups therefore is not simply to increase our knowledge of the Bible; it is to enable us to translate knowledge into action. Through small groups we grow in our experience of God, our obedience to Jesus as his disciples, and in the use of our gifts and our ministry to one another. There is a sharing of needs and a commitment to meeting those needs, both practically and in prayer. All this flows out of the deepening of relationships, which small groups make possible.

The church grows when it is built on the foundation of strong, healthy relationships. Small groups are essential to introducing new members to friends in the church, and to enabling lasting relationships to be maintained. Christianity in the twenty-first century is primarily relational. It is about relationship with God and relationships with people. This is what postmodern society is hungry for. This is the future of the church. The primary purpose of the church in the West at this time is to create community with Christ at the centre. It will be primarily through belonging and through relationships rooted in the love and mercy of God that the postmodern generation will find faith in Christ.

5

A Passion for Unity

Jesus had a passion for unity in his church. As Jesus prayed for the church in John 17:20–21 he cried out to the Father, 'I ask not only on behalf of these, but also on behalf of those who will believe in me through their word, *that they may all be one*.' Paul too was passionate about unity in the church. In 1 Corinthians 1:10 he speaks from his heart to the church in Corinth, saying:

> Now I appeal to you, brothers and sisters, by the name of our Lord Jesus Christ, that all of you should be in agreement and that there should be no divisions among you, but that you should be united in the same mind and the same purpose.

If the church is to have a transforming impact upon society, then it has to discover a passion for unity. Nothing else will do, because a divided church is a living denial of the reconciling work on the cross of the one Lord Jesus Christ.

Paul, writing about the division between Jews and Gentiles, says:

But now in Christ Jesus you who once were far off have been brought near by the blood of Christ. For he is our peace; in his flesh he has made both groups into one and has broken down the dividing wall, that is, the hostility between us. He has abolished the law with its commandments and ordinances, so that he might create in himself one new humanity in place of the two, thus making peace, and might reconcile both groups to God in one body through the cross, thus putting to death that hostility through it. (Ephesians 2:13–16)

Christ has broken down the dividing wall of hostility which otherwise keeps us apart. The reconciling love of Jesus brings unity and peace, healing and wholeness to a broken and divided world. This is why division in the church, and among Christians, is such a scandal. If the churches themselves are not reconciled, how can we expect the world to take seriously the gospel of reconciliation that we preach?

Unity in the church is a prerequisite for a spiritual breakthrough for the gospel in a city or community. Many mission organisations such as African Enterprise will not commit themselves to being involved in a mission to a town or city unless there is a 'critical mass' of unity and agreement among the churches and denominations. If there is not a substantial level of unity and co-operation, then the churches will be encouraged first to build bridges of reconciliation and agreement among themselves before seeking to present the gospel to the city in a major public initiative.

In some communities in various parts of the world where churches are committing themselves to reconciliation and to united prayer, remarkable changes are being reported. These transformed communities are not yet common but according to research conducted by George Otis Jr, and described in the *Transformations* video, they are growing in number.

Unity among the churches in a city or community is a powerful force for change, and sometimes it can make all the difference. A weak, divided church often finds itself preaching largely to its own members. A church that is united and involved with the community is able to make an impact far beyond its own immediate circle of influence. This is the transformation effect: the transforming church touching and changing the whole life of the community, through the release in new and extraordinary ways of the Holy Spirit.

This is what has happened in the city of Cali in Colombia. The pastors of many denominations in this city of over two million began all-night prayer vigils in May 1995 to take a stand against the drug cartels and the corruption that pervaded every institution in the city. Dr Ruth Ruibal and her husband Julio, of the Ekklesia Christian Colombian Center in Cali, were involved in the leadership of these prayer vigils. After receiving threats on his life, Julio was killed in December 1995. Following his death there has been a dramatic awakening in the church in Cali, which has led to a breaking down of denominational barriers in the city. This is Ruth Ruibal's testimony:

> The Lord allowed my husband, Julio C. Ruibal, to be a martyr for the gospel of Jesus Christ. Through natural eyes one would see it as a tragedy – losing a young man with a powerful apostolic ministry that has affected whole nations in South America. However, it was at his funeral that the most important event in the history of our city, Cali, took place – the pastors made a covenant of unity: we were one body and we would not allow anything to come between us or divide us. That covenant made over four years ago stands today. As a result we are seeing our city turned around.
>
> Just a few years ago, Cali was infamous for its drug trafficking and violence. The Cali cartel was acclaimed by the USA to

be the most powerful criminal organisation in the world. As we saw society deteriorate under corruption and injustice, the church began to meet together to pray all night. The first meeting, in March 1995, was held in the coliseum with about 20,000 people attending. It was then that we experienced the effect that prayer could have upon a city. That weekend taught us that united prayer could change a community: there were no violent deaths and just a few days later the first drug lord fell.

Now, as the church is strengthened by years of prayer and unity, we are seeing the results. Not only has the number of churches increased, but the number of evangelical Christians has doubled as well. Discipling the new converts is one of the most pressing problems in the church. Now the evangelical church is recognised by the civil authorities as an important segment of the community and Christians are addressing the problems in society. Following Cali's example, other cities in Colombia have begun all-night prayer vigils as well. It is through the united church, praying and working together, that we are seeing historical changes.[1]

One church

There is one body and one Spirit, just as you were called to the one hope of your calling, one Lord, one faith, one baptism, one God and Father of all, who is above all and through all and in all. (Ephesians 4:4–6)

The New Testament is absolutely clear: there is *one church*. We are so used to a multiplicity of denominations that we tend to assume that the norm is that there are many churches. Correspondingly we would not normally strategise

---

[1] Quoted in *Beyond 2000 – Community Transformation*, SOMA, Cape Town, November 2000 (conference booklet).

for the mission of the church in a city or town on the assumption that there is only one church, the church of the Lord Jesus Christ. We would think rather of the Baptists, the Presbyterians, the Roman Catholics, the Methodists, the Pentecostals and so on. It requires a radical shift of perspective to see the church as Jesus and the New Testament see it. We are so accustomed to division that we often assume it to be the norm. The desire of Jesus was unequivocally that his church would be one. He prayed:

> I ask not only on behalf of these, but also on behalf of those who will believe in me through their word, that *they may all be one*. As you, Father, are in me and I am in you, may they also be in us, so that the world may believe that you have sent me. The glory that you have given me I have given them, so that *they may be one*, as we are one, I in them and you in me, that *they may become completely one*, so that the world may know that you have sent me and have loved them even as you have loved me. (John 17:20–23)

One holy catholic and apostolic church

In the Nicene Creed we declare, 'We believe in *one* holy catholic and apostolic church.' There is one church, even though there are many denominations. The one church is the fellowship of all believers, all who believe and trust in the Lord Jesus Christ (Acts 13:39; Romans 10:9). Despite what appearances may indicate, this unity already exists. There is one family, because there is one Father; one faith because there is one Lord Jesus Christ, and one body because there is one Holy Spirit who gives life to the people of God. Because God is one, the church is one.

There is often value in having a number of different local churches in a community, with different styles of worship and witness. Some people prefer a quiet and meditative form of worship, others look for exuberance and excitement. One church may offer ritual and incense and colour, another may be plain and austere. One may be strong in proclamation and teaching, while another has a calling to the homeless or the street children. Diversity and difference is not a problem; on the contrary, diversity can be a huge asset where churches are willing to work together for the greater service of the kingdom.

But when there is division, or empire-building, or criticism of that which is not 'our way of doing things', then the transforming power of the gospel is hindered. God longs for unity among his people. He blesses unity, and through unity the kingdom of God is able to grow and spread through our communities, towns and cities.

When I was a pastor in Hilton, South Africa, we had a strong and committed fellowship among the clergy and pastors in our area. We agreed that our mission to the unchurched people of Hilton would be strengthened if we knew who belonged to one or another of our churches, and who had no church affiliation that any of us was aware of. So we pooled our membership lists, and created a new combined membership list that showed all those who were members of the one church, the holy catholic apostolic church in Hilton, which comprised Anglican, Methodist, Baptist, Roman Catholic, Assembly of God and Church of England in South Africa, as well as a few others who worshipped in other churches outside the local area.

We then committed ourselves to honouring one another, and to respecting the authority of each pastor over their own members. We agreed not to become involved in ministry to anyone who belonged to another local church without first consulting their own pastor. And we also committed ourselves to the goal of working together to reach those in the community who were not, as far as we knew, members of any of our churches. I am certain that God was honoured by this agreement, and that blessing and fruitfulness were released to the community through it.

The Nicene Creed also reminds us that we believe in one *holy* catholic apostolic church. To be holy means to be set apart, different and distinctive from the world. People must be able to see that we belong to God because we live holy and godly lives. The church must always have holiness even though it is not fashionable or popular.

And, we believe in one holy *catholic* apostolic church. The word 'catholic', according to the Oxford English Dictionary, means 'universal, all embracing, of wide sympathies'. If I have a catholic taste in music, I like everything from rock and jazz to classical and opera. When we say that we believe in one holy catholic church, we mean the all-embracing inclusive church, which includes all Christian believers from Greek or Russian Orthodox to Quakers and neo-Pentecostals.

Finally, we believe in one holy catholic *apostolic* church. The apostolic church is founded upon the teaching of the apostles, which is contained in the holy Scriptures. And the Bible, the apostolic teaching, defines that which is truly Christian. Groups such as the Jehovah's Witnesses, the Mormons and the Christian Scientists are not regarded as part of the one holy catholic apostolic church because they have altered or added to the apostolic teaching. But those who acknowledge and believe the holy Scriptures as containing 'sufficiently all doctrine required of necessity for eternal salvation through faith in Jesus Christ'[1] are one in Christ, and are all members of his one holy catholic apostolic church.

---

[1] *Book of Common Prayer*, Articles of Religion.

'Apostolic' also means 'sent', from the Greek word *apostello*, 'to send forth'. Jesus said, 'As the Father has sent me, so I send you' (John 20:21). The apostolic church is sent out by Jesus to proclaim the kingdom of God in word and deed.

The road to Rustenburg

One of the most remarkable stories of unity and reconciliation in the Christian church happened in South Africa in the years and months leading up to the historic democratic elections in April 1994. For a number of years prior to these elections there had been much painstaking work of bringing together Christian leaders from various backgrounds and denominations in order to foster a spirit of greater understanding and reconciliation within the South African church. Events such as the Durban Congress on Mission and Evangelism (1973), the South African Christian Leadership Assembly (1979) and the National Initiative for Reconciliation (1985) all played their part. This process was based upon the vision of establishing relationships between Christian leaders as a significant step towards bringing about a wider process of healing and reconciliation in the country.

During the time of negotiations leading up to the first fully democratic elections in 1994, it became increasingly clear that if the church was to play a significant role during the transition to democracy, it needed to be able to speak with one voice. Accordingly a conference was called at Rustenburg in the Eastern Transvaal in November 1990. The conference brought together an astonishingly wide spectrum of representatives and leaders from the whole Christian constituency in the nation.

The preamble to the Rustenburg Declaration, issued at the end of this extraordinary conference, declares:

We 230 (this number includes overseas guests from church bodies in various countries) representatives of 97 denominations and 40 organisations participating in the National Conference of Church Leaders in South Africa, have come together in Rustenburg in the belief that it is under the authority of God's Word and the guidance of the Holy Spirit that we meet. We have been convinced anew of God's amazing grace by the way in which, despite our wide variety of backgrounds, we have begun to find one another and to discover a broad consensus through worship, prayer, confrontation, confession and costly forgiveness. We have sought a spirit of patience, mutual care and openness as we have tried to discern the mind of Christ and have often been surprised how our views on many issues have converged. Some of us are not in full accord with everything said in this conference, but on this we are all agreed, namely the unequivocal rejection of apartheid as a sin. We are resolved to press forward in fellowship and consultation towards a common mind and programme of action.[1]

What this document represents is the church in the nation speaking with one voice. The conference was named the 'National Conference of Churches in South Africa'. It was in many ways a unique event, and the Rustenburg Declaration remains a powerful and significant prophetic document, which is relevant not only for South Africa, but for the church in many other nations. In many ways this declaration laid the foundation spiritually for the political miracle that took place less than four years later: the largely peaceful transition to a democratically elected government, with Nelson Mandela as President.

The conference arose out of an appeal by the then president F. W. de Klerk for the church in South Africa to formulate a

---

[1] Rustenburg Declaration, NIR, Pretoria 1990.

strategy conducive to negotiation, reconciliation and change. This was a time of crisis in the life of the nation. After the long years of apartheid, the possibility of a just and democratic society was at last emerging. But what kind of society would South Africa become? And how would the transition take place? At that time nobody knew. The churches were in the position where either they got their act together, and played the key role that was required of them, or they remained divided and ineffective, and thus failed God and the nation in its hour of need.

The conference itself was marked by a spirit of confession and a desire to find one another across the divides of history, doctrine and past misunderstanding. At one point Professor Willie Jonker, a theologian from Stellenbosch University, made a declaration that was both a personal confession and a confession in the name of the Dutch Reformed Church and the Afrikaner people. He said:

> I confess before you and before the Lord, not only my own sin and guilt, and my personal responsibility for the political, social, economic and structural wrongs that have been done to many of you, and the results of which you and our whole country are still suffering from, but *vicariously* I dare also to do that in the name of the Dutch Reformed Church (DRC) of which I am a member, and for the Afrikaner people as a whole. I have the liberty to do just that, because the DRC at its latest synod has declared apartheid a sin and confessed its guilt of negligence in not warning against it and distancing itself from it long ago.[1]

After Jonker's statement there were mixed feelings among a number of the delegates. How were they to respond to a

---

[1] Quoted in Michael Cassidy, *A Witness for Ever* (London: Hodder & Stoughton, 1995), p. 98.

confession like this? But Archbishop Desmond Tutu took
the initiative. He went to the lectern and said:

> Our brother here has asked for forgiveness for his sins and those
> of his church and people, and I believe it appropriate at this time
> that I should on behalf of black people who suffered so much
> under apartheid, express that we have heard this request for for-
> giveness, and from our hearts we extend our forgiveness and we
> say that we love you and we receive you and we put the past
> behind us.[1]

This amazing demonstration of Christ-centred confession, forgiveness and reconciliation made an enormous
impact upon the conference. The Rustenburg Conference,
and its declaration, prepared the way for what was to happen
in the nation politically, and indeed for the work of the Truth
and Reconciliation Commission later on. The church is
given by God the responsibility to set the spiritual foundations for the nations. We should not underestimate the spiritual influence and power in the nation of an obedient and
united church. It has been said that the church gets the
government it deserves. An obedient church will be a transforming church, a church that brings the values and the
power of the kingdom of God to the whole of society.

But there is a cost. Division is a cancer in the life of the
church. Before the church can arise and play its full and God-
given role in the nations it must be willing to seek reconciliation within its own constituent parts and groupings.
Reconciliation cannot be bought cheaply. Issues from the
past need to be dealt with, through confession and forgiveness. Dealing with our history is a prerequisite to unlocking

---

[1] *Ibid.*

a new future for the church, and, therefore, for the nation. Facing the past for many people can be very difficult and painful. But it must be done. Where there are continuing consequences of things that have happened that should not have happened, between bishops and clergy, between pastors and their people, between one church and another, there is work to be done. It is the work of Christ, the work of the cross. 'He is our peace, who has made us both one, and has broken down the dividing wall of hostility' (Ephesians 2:14 RSV).

Our unity must go beyond those with whom we have a large measure of agreement and must include those we differ from in many ways. We have to ask, 'Do we appear to serve different lords or the same Lord?' If Jesus is our common Lord then we should be working together. If we deny our common allegiance to the lordship of Jesus by all pulling in different directions, then our deeds deny our confessions, and our prayers are not able to break the powers and principalities that bind our communities.

The experience of the church in Cambridge

When I moved to Cambridge in September 1994 I soon discovered that the church in the city was deeply divided. Many church leaders and pastors did not know the names of the leaders and clergy in other churches, even those who lived and worked within a mile or two of their own church. Those who were not like-minded were often not meeting together at all.

At around the same time that I arrived in Cambridge a number of other new appointments in various churches in and around the city took place. I started to look for other pastors and leaders with whom I could meet for fellowship, prayer and mutual encouragement. I soon discovered that a number of people had been praying for some years for a new breakthrough of unity in the church in Cambridge.

Early in 1995 I was asked to speak to a meeting of the Cambridge Prayer Network about the process of reconciliation that had taken place among churches and church leaders in South Africa prior to the 1994 elections. As a result of this meeting, and the growing sense of urgency and concern about the division among the churches in Cambridge, a number of meetings were held in order to address these issues. A number of evangelical leaders, including myself, made a commitment to work together and to honour and respect one another's ministries. We began to hold combined citywide celebration events on Sunday evenings, called 'City Praise'. These were owned and led by the City Praise group of leaders, representing a wide spectrum of evangelical churches in and around Cambridge.

On Easter Sunday evening in 1997 the City Praise leaders held a celebration service of Holy Communion, in Holy Trinity Church in the centre of Cambridge. At this service we formally covenanted with one another to work together in unity in the name of the Lord Jesus Christ. We committed ourselves to the following:

1. To honour and respect one another, and one another's ministry, by discouraging gossipers, critics and 'church-hoppers'.
2. To pray for one another – in a committed, informal way.
3. To meet with one another – on a regular basis for mutual support, prayer and co-ordinated planning.
4. To promote and encourage one another's ministries – by sharing expertise, publicity and 'good reports'.
5. To encourage our congregations and organisations to work together in service, witness and the sharing of

resources. We see this to be an exciting opportunity for effective collaboration for the sake of the gospel.

The City Praise leaders' group then decided to widen our base and strategy and was renamed Christian Ministry Network (CMN). We have continued to meet regularly, to pray together, for one another and for the city. The core leadership have from time to time gone to a retreat centre away from Cambridge for 24 hours, to pray and seek the Lord together, and to deepen our fellowship and commitment to one another.

In 1997 I was asked by our bishop to head up the planning and preparation for the celebration of the Millennium in the Anglican Church in our region. As a result of this responsibility I became involved in a number of Millennium-related projects in Cambridge. I was a member of the Greater Cambridge Millennium Association, which brought together leaders from business, the universities, the city council and local authorities, and the churches. I was asked by the events manager of the Cambridge City Council to participate in the planning of a major Millennium event on Parker's Piece in Cambridge on the night of 31 December 1999. This event was expected to attract in the region of 40,000 people, which, in fact, it did. The city council recognised that there was an important Christian dimension to the celebration of the Millennium, as the 2,000th anniversary of the birth of Christ, and wanted the churches to participate in the Millennium Eve event.

But at that time there was no forum or meeting that included the leaders of all the major churches and denominations in Cambridge. When I asked the bishop about his willingness to participate in the event as a regional leader representing the wider Christian church, he told me that he would not feel able to do this unless he knew that he had the support of the churches in the city. But there was no means at that time to obtain a clear indication of this support. The CMN group was an evangelical group that included a large number of churches, but an equally large number of non-evangelical churches were not part of CMN, and were not participating in the @2000 mission.

I spoke to the Anglican archdeacon in Cambridge, Jeff Watson, and we together called a meeting of a wide spectrum of church leaders, including the leaders of all major groups and denominations. I presented to them the request from the city council for the church in Cambridge to work in partnership with themselves, the business community and the university in planning Cambridge's Millennium celebrations. The meeting unanimously agreed that this was an opportunity we could not afford to miss.

Millennium Eve was an unforgettable occasion. The *Cambridge Evening News* said:

Thousands enjoy Millennium revels in heart of city.
Up to 40,000 people crammed on to Parker's Piece in Cambridge to see in the new Millennium. As midnight approached, the Bishop of Huntingdon, the Rt Rev John Flack, read the Millennium Resolution and a big screen showed Big Ben as it chimed in the new year. The night climaxed with a spectacular firework display.

For nearly an hour leading up to midnight on 31 December 1999 on the main stage there was singing by a Black Gospel choir, with prayers and readings led by the bishop and a group of Christians, young and old, from the city of Cambridge. A large birthday cake, celebrating the 2,000th birthday of Jesus, was cut by a group of homeless people from a nearby church-run night shelter. Two large beacons signifying 'Jesus the Light of the World', and sponsored by the churches of Cambridge, were lit by the bishop and other local Christians. An on-site counselling and support service called the 'Listening Ear' was staffed by 25 local Christians on the most antisocial evening of the year to be working.

Since Millennium Eve there have been further significant opportunities for public working together for the churches in Cambridge. At Pentecost 2000 a large service of celebration was held in Great St Mary's, the largest church in Cambridge. Groups of Christians converged on the centre of Cambridge, walking in procession with flags and banners and musical instruments from the four corners of the city: north, south, east and west. The service contained contributions from a wide range of different church traditions and backgrounds, Protestant and Catholic, Pentecostal and reformed, traditional and modern. It was glorious!

Since then further public services and events have taken place, including a service, again at Great St Mary's, to mark the 800th anniversary of the grant by King John of a charter that created the first form of local government in Cambridge. Many senior civic dignitaries, as well as leaders from the universities and local business and commerce, attended and supported this service. During the service the contribution of the Christian church to the history of Cambridge was related, thanks were given to God for the past 800 years, and prayers were said for the future of the city and all its people. A clear message was presented of a church able to put aside past differences and speak with one voice on a major public occasion for the city.

Unity is powerful. It is powerful because it leads directly to mission. A united church is a transforming church, a church able to speak in word and deed to the community about a faith and an ethical foundation for life that is ours in Christ Jesus. Why did Jesus pray that his church should be one? It was not simply for the sake of the church and its people, but so that the world may believe that the Father has sent his Son and has loved them with the same love that he loved his own Son Jesus (see John 17:23). This is the transforming church in action; the transforming church that makes Jesus known to the world, in deed and in truth.

There is still much work to be done in Cambridge. We have begun to see that communities and cities can be changed by the power of God, working through a united, prayerful and obedient church. But persevering leadership is required, and there are many obstacles along the way. We know, however, that God is at work in new and exciting ways to bring transformation to our communities and our nations. This is the new vision of mission that God is giving to his church for the twenty-first century.

6

Serving the Community and Caring for the Poor

I recently met a person whom I had known briefly some years before when I was the pastor at a church in South Africa. I didn't recognise her at first, and neither did she recognise me. But after a short conversation light dawned. 'You visited my father before he died,' she said. 'Yes,' I said. 'I took his funeral. I remember it well.' The visit I had paid to the hospital to see her father, just before he died, was one of those unforgettable moments that God sometimes puts together in the life of a pastor. A door opened for a man who knew he was dying, a man unaccustomed to praying with someone else. I was there, and we prayed together, and soon afterwards he died. I was given the privilege of being there with him for those very significant few minutes, right at the end of his life.

This is something of what it means for me to be an ordained minister of the gospel. It's easy to get the wrong idea of what ordination is all about. At seminary or theological college there is training in doctrine, pastoral psychology, church history, liturgy and so on. In many suburban churches these days the clergy seem to spend their time going from meeting to meeting, and from programme to programme. Every day of the week there seems to be something happening, and the clergy or pastors are the ones who have the responsibility for planning and overseeing these programmes. But is this really what it's all about?

In the years shortly after my own ordination I came to a clear conviction that God has essentially called me to do three things:

- to pray
- to pastor God's people
- to preach and teach God's word

There are of course other things that need to be done, such as chairing the church council or board meeting. But I believe that I am called by God to three primary tasks – to pray, to pastor and to preach – and everything else is dependent on these three.

This is a model of church that is, under God, centred not on the organisation, or even on the minister, but on the people. A healthy church is a church where people are cared for, where they are noticed, and listened to. We have a goal that in our church no church members should slip through the net of pastoral care if they are in any kind of pastoral need. We aim to be in touch on a regular basis with all those who are members of our church.

Of course one pastor working alone cannot do this unless the church is tiny. What is needed is a team. We have a pastoral care team that meets for around two hours every week. We pray together, we share our needs and concerns, and we consider all the pastoral needs we are aware of in the congregation. Our aim is to ensure that everyone who is in need is followed up and cared for.

I cannot possibly do all the pastoral care myself. But in every church there are those to whom God has given a gift of caring, of visiting, of helping. Once those gifts are recognised and affirmed, they can be developed and greatly used by God. Training, encouragement and recognition all help enormously.

In our Anglican parish we not only have a responsibility to care for those who are our members, but we, like many other churches, see ourselves as having a calling from God to offer pastoral care to the whole community. No individuals will be turned away if they come to us in need, regardless of their background or difficulty. There are so many ways in which an active and caring church can reach out to their local community with the love of Christ. This is mission: it is the love of Jesus in action, and the need for this is as great today as it ever has been.

A good place to begin is to compile an inventory of your local community. Write down all the different groups and organisations that are present. Some of these will already have some point of contact with the local church; others none at all. The list may include such groups as parents and toddlers, children, teenagers, retired people, the housebound, the bereaved, the sick and so on. Wherever opportunities arise to reach out and build relationships, be ready to grasp them. We encourage members of our church to be part of organisations like the day centre for the elderly or the local community youth club, and to build opportunities for contact with the church.

Our church has had a particular concern over a number of years for parents and toddlers. We have many of these in our community, with between 60 and 80 babies being born each year in Milton. Sue Nunn, one of our pastoral visitors, has been the key person in enabling much of this work to

happen. I asked Sue how she had become involved with
parents and toddlers:

Ian   Sue, how did you become involved with parents and
toddlers at All Saints Church?

Sue   It was after I had left work, and I felt that there was a
need. There was a gap at that time, so I just came
along.

Ian   This is something where you clearly have found your
niche, isn't it? It's something where you are in your
element.

Sue   Yes. I enjoy it because I enjoy being with young children as well as caring for their parents, mostly mothers,
but there is the occasional father, and childminders as
well. It's because I love children. I just love people.

Ian   We see lots and lots of mums, and dads sometimes,
with their little children, many of whom have no other
contact with the church.

Sue   No. None at all. Some in fact do come to church at
Christmas and Easter, and there is the Starting Blocks
service once a month, which we try to persuade them
to join. But many obviously do not, so the toddler
group is the only contact that they have with the
church and with Christianity. We just hope that by our
example, and by the love and care we give them, we are
sowing seeds and building bridges, and one day they
may come to the Lord. I feel that my role is just
Christian caring, and although the Christian part is
extremely important, the caring is in some ways what
we are about.

Ian   Yes, I think that is very important, and it helps them
to see that the church is a safe place, a place which they
could come to if they have a need.

Sue   Absolutely. And I do visit, and hopefully we do pick up on needs. If there is an extra need, I do home visits and care for them that way. When new babies are born there is great interest, and baptism is often a follow-up to that from the baby group.

Ian   How do you keep going? You have been doing this for a long time now.

Sue   I did actually leave some years ago and I came back, because I missed it so much. I felt that the Lord was still telling me to do it. Also I get some extra help and we changed the system, and it was easier. But I do get very weary, and sometimes I just wish I hadn't got to go. But I have wonderful support, and kitchen support from the older folks. There is a wonderful team of church people, so there is great back-up from everybody.

Ian   It does certainly help in the way that the church is perceived in the whole of the community. For instance, when we have services like Christingle or the Starting Blocks service on Christmas Eve, we are always amazed how many people come. There are people that we would not see at any other time of the year, and many of these are young parents who feel that it is important at least at that time of the year to come to church.

Sue   Yes, absolutely, and a lot of the baby mums were extremely keen to come this year, which is absolutely brilliant.

Ian   Starting Blocks has been important, because that is now a regular monthly service. Can you describe Starting Blocks for us?

Sue   It's a service for pre-school children and we have a theme and a programme. Last week it was about giving thanks and we did the story of the ten lepers. It's very simple and lasts for about 20 minutes. We have two of the same songs each time, and then appropriate songs to the theme. Then we go into the hall and do craft, which is also on the theme, and the mums chat and have a cup of tea. The children love it because it is very simple and at their level. The mums enjoy bringing the children and we have an opportunity to talk to the mums over a cup of tea. And it has just grown. It's been great and again it's been fun. We have all sorts of different people on the team, some who are only slightly connected to the church, like mums whose toddlers have now gone to school, and who are happy to help out.

Ian   You have discovered your own ministry in all this, haven't you?

Sue   Oh yes, absolutely. Sometimes I think I could be doing something different but I really enjoy this and I think it does me good. I just feel that the Lord wants me to do it. My daughter tells me I should retire when I'm 60, but I don't think so.

Ian   Well, I know from talking to people who have been part of mums and toddlers in the past, and who perhaps have even moved away from Milton, that when I ask them about the church, they say, 'Oh, Sue Nunn.' You are the first person they think of when they remember Milton Church. I think that's wonderful.

The church that takes people seriously is concerned with ordinary people, and with meeting their needs, even in simple and non-risky ways. This, however, does not mean it is not costly, or that it does not require commitment. What people like Sue Nunn do is costly, but it makes a real difference to people's lives.

This ministry of caring and serving others builds bridges that enable people to come into the life of the church, the Christian community. It also presents very simple models of church life and worship, such as the Starting Blocks services, which are accessible to people with little or no church background.

The homeless

Our work with parents and toddlers has enabled us to support and care for mums, and sometimes dads, with babies and small children in a wide variety of needs and circumstances. But there are others in our cities and communities who find themselves in a truly desperate state. Homelessness has become a major problem in Britain. People become homeless for many reasons. Often it is a combination of mental illness, relationship breakdown, drink and drugs, and other factors. The consequence of these difficulties for some people in this society is that they find themselves sleeping rough on the streets, or in a car park, or under a bridge somewhere. For most of them, their problems are immense. But a church that cares about people will surely care about people who are homeless.

In Cambridge, Jimmy's Night Shelter at the Zion Baptist Church provides a home every night of the year for 25 men and 6 women (and up to 2 dogs) who find themselves in this position. Each year around 400 different people are accommodated at Jimmy's. Some stay there for several months, but most only stay a few nights. The night shelter is named after Jim, who was a resident of the former winter-only temporary night shelter in Cambridge. Jim spent much of his life living rough. When he died a small group of people decided to work together to establish a permanent all-year shelter for the homeless in Cambridge. In the winter of 1995 Jimmy's Night Shelter was born, and its work has grown and developed since then. There are now over 200 trained volunteers who support the work that is based around Jimmy's. There is a community transport service called Dial-a-Ride for the elderly and disabled. Some of Jimmy's guests make up a football team called the Zion Eagles, who play in a local league, and who recently took part in a national five-a-side tournament.

Working with the homeless is not easy. Every Friday at Zion Baptist a free lunch is provided for the homeless and anyone else who wants to drop in. The food is good, the service is excellent, and the company is always interesting. Many of those who come to Jimmy's have complex and difficult histories. When I arrived, one of the helpers said to me, 'Don't leave anything lying around – it might disappear.' I looked at him. 'Stuff gets nicked,' he said. 'We get some good ones, and some not so good.' He told me about the problem of the blankets that get left halfway down the street, instead of being brought back to the shelter.

The people who come to Jimmy's are, by and large, life's casualties. Tony Barker is the Baptist minister at Zion Church and his vision, commitment and leadership have been a key part of the development of Jimmy's. He said to me, 'We see the casualties at the sharp end. They are lovely people – all of them. But some are an absolute pain sometimes when they are drunk.'

I asked Tony about the large numbers of people offering themselves to work as volunteers at Jimmy's. He told me that on that morning alone they had received 25 applications from new volunteers. 'It's costly service,' he said, 'but it is blessed. Anyone who comes and volunteers will receive a blessing far above the service being given.' He turned to a woman who was helping with the food. 'Who told you to come here?' he asked. 'Was it Alan?'

'No,' she said.

'Was it Dominic?'

'No,' she said. 'It was God.'

Caring for the homeless is not easy or straightforward. It needs a lot of wisdom to run a place like Jimmy's. Our own local church tries to support and give encouragement to the work at Jimmy's, partly because it keeps us in touch with those who are serving some of the most needy people in our community. But Jimmy's is also a blessing to the whole body of Christ in Cambridge, because through Jimmy's much work is done that individual churches like ours would find difficult, as it takes expertise and commitment. Because of the problems, many people prefer to avoid doing the kind of work that Jimmy's does. Yet Tony Barker says, 'These are brilliant people who have taught us so much. Jesus said that foxes have holes and birds of the air have nests, but that the Son of Man has nowhere to lay his head. Sometimes in this place we have the feeling that we have touched the very hem of the garment of Christ.'

Caring for the poor

We live in the age of globalisation. In the developed world, standards of living have risen steadily for the past few decades. But most of the Christians in the world at the beginning of the twenty-first century are not affluent. Many live in poverty and deprivation. The church, the body of Christ, is a global family. Yet even as I write this, many of my brothers and sisters are hungry, and I have food to spare.

The statistics for global poverty are appalling. Half the people on earth live on less than two dollars a day. A billion people have less than a dollar a day to live on. This means that a billion people go to bed hungry every night.

We hear a great deal in the West about the information technology revolution. But at the end of the twentieth century there were more telephone lines in New York than in the whole of sub-Saharan Africa, and half of humanity had never made a telephone call. A quarter of all the people on earth never get a clean glass of water. One woman dies every minute in childbirth. This is the reality of our global village.

Yet the Bible tells us that all those who belong to Christ Jesus are one body. We are all brothers and sisters in Christ, whether we live in Mozambique, China, Brazil or Switzerland. We are the family of God, the body of Christ, the holy catholic church.

The New Testament has some challenging things to say to the rich Christians of the developed world at the beginning of the new millennium. John says, 'If any one has the world's goods and sees his brother or sister in need, yet closes his heart against him, how does God's love abide in him?' (1 John 3:17). And in the letter of James we read:

> What good is it, my brothers and sisters, if you say you have faith but do not have works? Can faith save you? If a brother or sister is naked and lacks daily food, and one of you says to them, 'Go in peace; keep warm and eat your fill', and yet you do not supply their bodily needs, what is the good of that? (James 2:14–16)

The affluent Christians of the West simply have to grasp this nettle if our discipleship is to have any integrity or credibility in the twenty-first century. We deliberately have to choose a different way of living, where we renounce luxury and follow Jesus. The Oxford English Dictionary defines luxury as: '**Luxury**. (Habitual use of) choice or costly food, dress, furniture, etc.; thing desirable but not indispensable.'

This is the challenge. We need to give up, for the sake of Jesus, the habitual use of choice or costly food, dress, furniture and the other expensive consumer items that are constantly being offered to us. It is time for Western Christians to turn away from luxury and to live simply, so that others may simply live. There are many things most of us would like to buy or to own, which are desirable but not indispensable. Let us bring our desires to Jesus, and lay them at the cross, and then we shall be free.

This does not mean that we never buy any expensive goods. Sometimes it is wiser to buy goods that are well made and that will last for a long time than to buy something cheap that will soon be broken and need replacing. A simple and disciplined way of life will be shown by its fruits. What we are aiming for is a life of freedom to obey and follow Christ, and a generosity in giving away to those in need the good things that God has given us. So let us be bold. Let us give away our riches, and learn to live in joy and contentment, holding on only to those things we really need. The rest can go, to bless the poor and to be used for the work of the kingdom of God. Only then will we have treasure in heaven, as Jesus promised (Matthew 6:20).

Globalisation and transformation

In many respects, at this point in history, it is the church in the developing world that is growing rapidly and that is strong in faith and discipleship. Christians in countries such as Sudan, Indonesia and the Democratic Republic of Congo are living out their faith in situations of severe difficulty and suffering. At the same time the church in the affluent and comfortable West is in widespread decline. In the twenty-first century, perhaps as never before, the church in the West needs the church in the developing world. The Western church has much to offer. It is rich in material resources, in theological education and in the depths of its spiritual inheritance. But it is also desperately needy. The truth is that in the worldwide church we need one another. Globalisation is a key issue just as much for the church as it is for the world of trade and business. In the West the church has to learn to care for Christians in the developing world, much more than we are doing at present. We also have to learn to receive from them, and to allow their insights and experience of the gospel to renew our own faith, witness and discipleship.

I am a South African. My wife, Alison, is English, and although we now live in England I regularly visit South Africa because I still have many close friends and family there. One Monday during a recent visit I spent the day with a friend of mine, Sarah Dottridge, and a 75-year-old Roman Catholic nun, Sister Joachim Buthelezi, visiting a very poor community in Sweetwaters, near Pietermaritzburg in Kwazulu Natal.

Sweetwaters is a densely populated semi-rural community, well off the beaten track. In Sweetwaters itself there is virtually no paid employment, although over 100,000 people live in the whole Sweetwaters area. Sarah, Sister Joachim and I spent most of the day with a group, mainly of women, who meet at an old Lutheran church in the Mbanjwa area. They crochet woollen blankets and make hats from old plastic shopping bags, which are collected by Sarah and sold through shops and other agencies in South Africa and in Canada. Most of these women have virtually no income at all, apart from what they earn through the blankets and hats. Some receive money from children who have grown up and have moved to the town where they have jobs. But many in the towns and cities are now dying of AIDS. Because of AIDS, the problem of poverty and starvation in the rural areas has become much worse. When parents in the town find they have AIDS they send their children back to the grannies and aunties in the rural areas, where there is no income. Many old widows find themselves trying to support eight or ten children, in tiny two- or three-bedroom huts and houses. Some have old-age pensions, but even the pension is only £30 to £40 per month. So people here are poor to the point of starvation, literally. And this is the picture of what life is like in much of sub-Saharan Africa.

Yet although these people are so poor, they have an enormous amount to give. There is much that we in the affluent West can learn from them. They know how to care for one another, even though they have so little. I visited one family who were being helped by Sarah and her group with regular food parcels. The husband in this family used to be a carpenter. In an accident his hand was cut off, and badly sewn on again. He is now unable to work, and at present this family have no income at all. The community were trying to help them by giving what they could. But the children were so hungry that they would take a tin plate and go round to their neighbours saying, 'Please give us some food.' So the community asked Sarah, 'Please can you help this family?' and she was able to provide food parcels for them.

Each Monday after the blankets and hats have been collected, and money paid out for them, the women queue up to buy cheap soup powder, tea, beans, sugar and soap, which are purchased in bulk and sold outside the church on Monday mornings. Then everyone goes into the church, and there is a time for singing and worship, for sharing of needs and concerns, for preaching and teaching, and for praying for one another. Time is not a big issue for the poor. No one is looking at their watch and thinking, 'I've got other things to do.' People here have time to meet and to care for one another as a community, and they have time for God. They know their need of one another, and they know their need of God. There are no social services, no one else to whom they can shift the responsibility of caring. The poor are humble, because they have no option. They do not have the problem of being tempted to put their trust in material wealth and human resources. They cry out to God, and they live in daily dependence upon him.

In the early years of the new millennium, 2,000 years (more or less) after the birth of Jesus, where do we find God now appearing to his people? God is God, and he chooses where and how he will make himself known. He has made himself known uniquely in Jesus Christ, and he still reveals himself in countless ways, to those who seek him, and sometimes to those who don't. But the Song of Mary in Luke 1:47–53 gives us a particular insight into God's priorities:

My soul magnifies the Lord,
    and my spirit rejoices in God my Saviour,
for he has looked with favour on the lowliness of his servant.
    Surely, from now on all generations will call me blessed;
for the Mighty One has done great things for me,
    and holy is his name.
His mercy is for those who fear him
    from generation to generation.
He has shown strength with his arm;
    he has scattered the proud in the thoughts of their hearts.
He has brought down the powerful from their thrones,
    and lifted up the lowly:
he has filled the hungry with good things,
    and sent the rich away empty.

The words of the Magnificat remind us of God's priorities, which are timeless. He is the God who scatters the proud, who calls the rich to share their wealth with the poor, and to whom those in power and authority are always accountable. At the same time we are reminded that God cares in a special way for the poor, the weak and the hungry.

Our God is the God who cares. He cares so much that he sent his only Son to be our Saviour. Unless the church cares as God cares and loves as God loves, we shall have no credibility in our claim to be servants of the Lord Jesus Christ.

> Christ has no body now on earth but ours,
> no hands but ours,
> no feet but ours.
>
> Ours are the eyes through
> which must look out Christ's
> compassion on the world.
>
> Ours are the feet with which
> he is to go about doing good.
>
> Ours are the hands with which
> he is to bless people now.
>   (Prayer of St Teresa)

PART 3

The Church Rooted in God

'You shall love the Lord your God with all your heart, and with all your soul, and with all your mind.' This is the greatest and first commandment.

(Matthew 22:37–38)

7

Worship and Liturgy

In the autumn of 2000, I was visiting Canada as part of three months' sabbatical leave from my church in Cambridge. I found myself staying in a hotel in Langley, near Vancouver in British Columbia. It was a Saturday night and I was wondering about finding a church to go to on Sunday morning. I remembered seeing somewhere that there was a Vineyard church in Langley that had produced a worship CD, so I found the phone number, picked up some directions and the time of service, and the next day headed down the road to worship.

The church was not easy to find. It didn't look like a church. It looked to me like a warehouse that had been converted to a hall and offices. The entrance was round the back, down an alleyway. By the time I found the entrance I was about 5 to 10 minutes late, but I soon realised that didn't matter at all. In the main hall a music group was playing, and they were good – very good. The congregation was mainly young adults very informally dressed, with quite a few children. People were still arriving after I got there. Some stood and worshipped, others sat, some children danced at the front. I soon became aware of a strong sense of the presence of God, and began to worship myself. This continued for some 40 minutes, with a relaxed informality and yet also an intensity and passion that affected me powerfully.

'I'm desperate for you,' the group sang. 'I'm lost without you.' And I knew they meant it. They weren't just singing the words. This church meant business with God.

The transforming church is serious about God. Increasingly I am meeting teenagers and younger adults who don't want to 'play church', and go through the motions of being religious or simply attending Sunday worship. At the New Wine summer camp in August 2000, a youth leader from Sheffield, Joanna Oyeniran, spoke powerfully to the gathering of some 5,000 people about the vision many Christians of her generation share. She said, 'The Lord wants us, like Joshua, to take the land, not just to visit. Our vision is to see the land changed, one person at a time. The kind of Christianity that young people are up for is one that believes that God heals, God saves, God does the business, that God will take the land. Like Shaftesbury, like Wesley, like Wilberforce. When people say, "Where is God?" we say, "He's right here," and "He's right now."'

This kind of passion for God is rooted in worship and prayer. When people are desperate for God, they are also serious about worship and about seeking the face of God. This means giving time to worship, not just an hour on Sunday morning before we go to the beach or go shopping. The whole service at Langley Vineyard on Sunday morning lasted over three hours (including a 20-minute break for coffee and doughnuts and meeting people).

Langley Vineyard is a church of the new generation, the informal culture of today. But it reminded me of a number of churches in Africa that I have attended, where there was a similar relaxed attitude to time and to people coming and going, while the worship went on, often for over three or four hours. In those churches in Africa there is also a seriousness about God, and about the gospel, and a sense that being in church and seeking God is *the* most important thing that people could be doing. When people know their need of God, when they are hungry for him, they will stay as long as they can so that they may simply know again and experience in their own lives the power of Jesus to heal and to save.

True worship is all about God. It is not primarily about music or forms of liturgy or the preacher. True worship begins with hearts that are desperate for God. As the psalmist says,

> Whom have I in heaven but You?
> And there is none upon earth
>   that I desire besides You.
> My flesh and my heart fail;
> But God is the strength of my
>   heart and my portion forever. (Psalm 73:25–26 NKJV)

True worship is rooted in this kind of longing for God, this awareness that our flesh and heart fail without God.

Jesus said, 'I am the vine, you are the branches. Those who abide in me and I in them bear much fruit, because apart from me you can do nothing' (John 15:5). This is a hard truth for us to grasp in our age that so prizes self-sufficiency and human achievement. But the truth is that if we are relying on our own strength to advance the kingdom of God, then we are bound to fail. We are utterly dependent on Jesus. Without him we can do nothing. Without him we can certainly not see a transformed nation, or even changed lives or renewed churches. So we must begin by coming to God in worship; worship that is real, worship that is serious about God and about seeking to enter his holy presence. Real worship comes from the heart, touches the whole of our being, and is expressed in our outward, active response.

So if we are to think about the transforming church, we must begin with worship. To experience true worship is to be transformed. Therefore any church that wishes to engage in bringing about transformation must begin by paying serious attention to its worship.

Integrity and reality

> But the hour is coming, and is now here, when the true worshippers will worship the Father in spirit and truth, for the Father seeks such as these to worship him. (John 4:23)

The key to true worship is that it must be authentic. The moment we get into putting on a show, then something begins to be lost in our worship. Of course we often find ourselves distracted and self-centred during times of worship. True worship is not about striving for perfection. It is about the intention of our hearts. We come to seek the living God in our humanity and weakness, but desiring with all our hearts to meet with him, on his terms, and by his grace alone.

In previous generations there was less pressure on the church to pay attention to public perception of its worship. Most people in the developed world today are constantly exposed to high-quality presentations of drama, music, ideas and opinions. So when they come to church, they will immediately begin to assess what they are seeing. The amount of care that has been taken in the preparation of the worship will be noticed, as will the skill and giftedness or otherwise of the worship leaders. But it is integrity and reality that speak loudest of all. If the worship is led by people who are willing to be real and to identify culturally and relevantly with their congregation, then that will make a huge difference to the impact of what is happening, especially to visitors.

True worship will never go out of fashion. The heart of true worship is timeless. But it must be clothed in forms of liturgy that are alive and relevant to the congregation.

What's it all about?

Christian worship is first of all about God. We come to worship in order to fix our attention on the one who is being worshipped: Almighty God, Father, Son and Holy Spirit.

This, then, is our message. It's all about God. When we come to worship, we come as God's people, to meet with the one who is Lord of all, to exalt him, to acknowledge him for who he is. The words 'church' and 'kirk' come from the Greek word *kyriakos*, which means 'belonging to the Lord'. So the priority as we prepare to worship must always be to place God at the centre.

This means that a sense of awe and reverence will always be present when God is being worshipped in spirit and in truth. After all, he is Almighty God, the Lord of time and eternity, the creator of heaven and earth. In Ecclesiastes 5:1–2 we are told, 'Guard your steps when you go to the house of God . . . for God is in heaven, and you upon earth; therefore let your words be few.'

The psalms tell us how to approach the presence of the Lord. We are to enter his courts with reverence and humility, with praise and thanksgiving. We are to come before him with a deep desire to seek his face, and to worship at his footstool (Psalms 99:5; 100:1–3).

The primary principle of worship is to fix our attention on the one being worshipped. This depends upon our knowing

God, and being mindful of who he is, and of his qualities and attributes. The book of Daniel gives us a striking example of what this means. King Nebuchadnezzar of Babylon had dreamed such dreams that his spirit was deeply troubled. He demanded that his magicians and wise men tell him both the dream and the interpretation, or they would all be put to death. They replied, quite understandably, that unless the king told them the dream, they could not give an interpretation.

Daniel then made an offer in order to save both his own life and the lives of the magicians and wise men. If the king gave him time he would tell the king the dream and the interpretation. He then went to his home and asked his companions, Hananiah, Mishael and Azariah to seek mercy from the God of heaven concerning this mystery, so that Daniel and his companions and the rest of the wise men of Babylon might not perish. So they cried out to God, and God revealed the mystery to Daniel in a vision. And we are told that Daniel worshipped God, and his worship was completely focused, not on his own need and situation, but on the character, qualities and attributes of God. Daniel said:

> Blessed be the name of God from age to age,
>   for wisdom and power are his.
> He changes times and seasons,
>   deposes kings and sets up kings;
> he gives wisdom to the wise
>   and knowledge to those who have understanding.
> He reveals deep and hidden things;
>   he knows what is in the darkness,
>   and light dwells with him.
> To you, O God of my ancestors,
>   I give thanks and praise,

for you have given me wisdom and power,
and have now revealed to me what we asked of you,
for you have revealed to us what the king ordered.

(Daniel 2:20–23)

For Daniel, even in a position of great personal danger, prayer and worship was centred totally on God, on who he is and on his power to transform any situation. Daniel knew his God, and his knowledge of God was centred in worship and prayer. Daniel knew that God is the Lord of time and history, that he raises up and casts down rulers and kings and governments. He is indeed a great and mighty God; nothing, absolutely nothing, is too difficult for him. No situation is beyond his saving and healing power.

Worship depends on knowing God

Unless we know God, we cannot worship. How can we know God? The Bible says that we can know him in a number of ways. We can see the glory of God revealed in his creation (Psalm 19:1) and his ways of righteousness and truth revealed in all that he has made (Romans 1:18–20). But above all we can know him in his Son Jesus Christ, the one who is God with us, Emmanuel, who came to save his people from their sins (Matthew 1:21). By turning from our sins, and putting our trust in the Lord Jesus Christ, the promise of Scripture is that we can know God: 'Therefore, since we are justified by faith, we have peace with God through our Lord Jesus Christ' (Romans 5:1).

Daniel was a man who knew God, whose life was rooted through prayer and worship in an intimate, daily, personal relationship with the God of all creation. This kind of relationship with God is only possible through faith. It is not about an academic study of the attributes of God. When we see by faith who God is and know in our own experience his saving and healing power and love, then we will begin to worship God. Without faith it is impossible to worship God.

Worship is a response to the revelation of God

Christian worship is a response to the revelation of God. God has above all revealed himself and spoken to us through his Son, Jesus. The church over many centuries has known that there are three further means through which God chiefly chooses to reveal himself to his people. These are the Holy Spirit, the word of God, and the sacraments.

The *Holy Spirit* is the third person of the Holy Trinity, God in us. He is the Lord, the giver of life. He is called by Jesus the Counsellor, the Helper, the Comforter, the one who leads us into all truth. He convicts us of sin and reveals to us the righteousness of God. He makes Jesus real to us. Jesus said, 'He will glorify me, because he will take what is mine and declare it to you' (John 16:14).

It is the Holy Spirit who gives life to the church. A church that resists the Holy Spirit, or that even stops being open to the Spirit, will soon start to become formalised and lacking in vitality. On the other hand, when the Holy Spirit is welcomed, and when his gifts and ministries are encouraged, the church will surely grow in spiritual strength, in Christlikeness and, usually, in numbers. God makes himself known and reveals his will and purposes for his people primarily through the work of the Holy Spirit in his church.

The *word of God* is the Bible, the canonical holy Scriptures, which 'uniquely reveal the word of God and contain all things necessary for eternal salvation through Jesus

Christ'.[1] Time and again God's people have found that he has chosen to make himself known through the written word of the Bible. Somehow, in a mysterious but unmistakable way, God speaks to his church through this book as he does through no other book. Above all, the apostolic Christian faith, as revealed to the first apostles and passed on by them to the early church, is authoritatively and definitively passed from one generation to the next in the pages of the Bible.

So God is revealed when his word is read and proclaimed. The psalms were central to the worship of Jesus, together with the rest of the Old Testament Scriptures. Today the Christian church still roots its worship in the Bible, through liturgy, through preaching, through songs and canticles and choruses, because we know that God will speak when his word, the Bible, is given its proper authority, when it is revered and obeyed.

A *sacrament* is defined in the Anglican catechism as 'an outward and visible sign of an inward and spiritual grace'.[2] The two primary sacraments of the church are baptism and Holy Communion. Baptism is the sacrament of initiation into Christ through a washing or cleansing with water. Holy Communion is the ongoing nourishment of grace to live the Christian life, with bread and wine as the outward signs of the spiritual food of the body and blood of Christ. Both of these are received in obedience to the teaching of the Bible, and have been part of the church's life since the earliest days of the book of Acts. Baptism and Holy Communion are essential to the life and worship of any church that is seeking to be obedient to Christ. Why, for example, do we take Holy

---

[1] Anglican Prayer Book, Church of the Province of Southern Africa.
[2] *Ibid.*

Communion? At a very simple level, it is because this is what Jesus commanded us to do. He said, 'Do this in remembrance of me.' But it has been the experience of the church for 2,000 years that baptism and Holy Communion are powerful ways in which God reveals himself and sustains and feeds his people. Holy Communion in particular is a sacrament for the whole of life, the good times and the bad. It is the place where Jesus makes himself known, time and time again, as he did once on the Emmaus Road, in 'the breaking of the bread' (Luke 24:35).

It is interesting to reflect that the three main streams of Christianity in the twentieth century have been the Roman Catholic, the Protestant or evangelical, and the Pentecostal. Each of these places particular emphasis on one of the three means of revelation that I have just discussed. The Roman Catholic Church emphasises the sacraments, the Protestants and evangelicals place the Bible at the centre of church life, while the Pentecostals (and charismatics) are the people of Pentecost, who focus on the gifts and ministries of the Holy Spirit. But all three are needed for the growth and health of the whole church, the one true body of Christ.

Worship is the discipline of placing ourselves before God without preconditions, in order that we may meet with him. God reveals himself again and again to his people through his Holy Spirit, through the Bible, and in the sacraments of baptism and Holy Communion. So if we desire to come into the presence of God, these are the places where we need to go. We need to hunger and thirst for more of the Spirit of God. We need to place ourselves under his word, the Bible. And we need to be baptised, and to come regularly to Holy Communion.

Of course, worship consists of much more than just these three primary means of revelation. The Bible gives a great deal of instruction in true and acceptable worship, and the Psalms in particular are the prayer book (and worship book) of the Bible. Psalm 96:9 (NKJV) says, 'Oh, worship the LORD in the beauty of holiness!' We enter his presence with thanksgiving and praise (Psalms 95:1–2; 100). When God reveals himself to us, we recognise that we are unworthy, that we fall far short of his glory and his holiness (Isaiah 6:1–8). We need therefore to confess our sins, and to receive assurance of God's forgiveness towards us in Christ Jesus. When the church comes to worship we shall want to share family news, and to pray for one another and for the needs of the world. Sometimes time will be spent in quietness, waiting upon God, and listening to his still, small voice. For the Quakers, this is the central focus of their worship, in the 'meeting of friends'.

All these elements are important, and they all have their place and time. But how does the church work this out, especially in a time where there is a major shift of cultures?

In Christian worship, we have to ask, in our own time and culture: How do we best communicate what we are wanting to say? We do this through good liturgy. The Oxford English Dictionary defines liturgy as 'a form of public worship, especially in the Christian church'. A liturgy may be a set or written form of service, but there is a sense in which every church has a liturgy. For some churches it is a simple unwritten liturgy, but none the less it is 'a form of public worship'. The 'liturgy' may consist simply of a time of singing and praise, a reading from the Bible, a sermon or teaching, and a time for prayer or ministry. Other churches, which may describe themselves as 'liturgical', have an elaborate form of service, possibly ritualistic in style, with all or most of the service written down in a prayer book or service book.

Good liturgy

Worship may be formal or informal in style. It may use a written liturgy, or the 'liturgy' may be unwritten but none the less well understood and recognised by all the participants. Good liturgy, however, is rooted in the history and inheritance of the church, and enables the worshippers both to encounter God and to grow to maturity in their faith and discipleship. Good liturgy does not focus week after week on one or two aspects of Christian worship, and neglect the rest. It makes room for different aspects and emphases, because all are necessary for the whole body to grow to maturity. Various people in the church will bring differing gifts and strengths and concerns, and this is right and healthy. Good liturgy makes space for the whole body of Christ to meet together, to learn from one another, and to grow into a deeper knowledge and experience of God.

As an Anglican, I have come to value greatly the liturgical inheritance of the Anglican Church. The seasons of the Church's year from Advent to Christmas and Epiphany, from Lent to Holy Week and Easter, and then through Pentecost to Trinity, all provide a range of times and seasons God uses in different ways to speak to his people and to lead them on, week by week, year by year. The variety, the different colours used in different seasons, the times for fasting and the times for celebration, all these are a great gift, which I believe the Holy Spirit has given to the church. They are biblically rooted and have been tested and formed over generations of the church's life and witness.

Good Christian liturgy is always built on biblical foundations. Biblical canticles and psalms provide the core of most of the liturgies of the historic churches. But in addition to this, good liturgy enables the whole counsel of God to form and shape the worshipping life of the church. Good liturgy ensures that there is a time for thanksgiving and praise, a time for penitence and forgiveness, a time to pray and a time to listen, a time to mourn and a time to dance. Good liturgy gives us doctrinal wholeness and balance. It saves and protects God's people from the idiosyncrasies of their pastor or leader, from the preacher's pet subjects, and from the individual worshipper's own tendency to prefer a particular emphasis or doctrine or style of worship.

So the liturgies of the church have much that is of value. They keep us in touch with the inheritance of the church. They provide something stable and sure in times of dryness, in times when spontaneous personal expression before God does not seem appropriate or true to where we are in our own hearts before God. Many charismatic and Pentecostal churches have rejected a formal liturgical approach, and have tried to return to what they see as an authentic New Testament model. But all churches sooner or later end up with a liturgy of some sort. The key question is whether that liturgy leads to growth in godliness and spiritual maturity in the congregation, or whether in some ways it hinders that growth.

Worship in a new generation

The challenge for the church in this time of rapidly changing cultures is to produce forms of worship anchored in the biblical patterns of worship and the inheritance of the church, but also relevant to the informal and uncommitted generation of today. Ours is a generation that lives in the here and now, which is both patronising about the past and yet unable to discern the future, because the future is so unpredictable. So we keep our options open, focusing on the present reality, but all the time looking and longing for something less transient, something that makes sense of life, something eternal.

It is a generation looking for reality and integrity, both highly critical and yet profoundly concerned to make a difference. It is the *Friends* generation, for whom relationships matter, perhaps above all else. For many, relationships are the only sure thing they have. This is the generation of clubbing and backpacking, of Indie and the Internet, of Soul Survivor and Taizé. When Christians of this generation gather to worship, they will be looking for models of worship that speak to them, and to their worldview. Robed choirs and *Hymns Ancient and Modern* are unlikely to be relevant or appealing. In fact the only impact old-fashioned styles of worship are likely to have is to drive this generation away from the church.

The challenge for the transforming church is to allow its outward forms of worship to be flexible and dynamic in order to speak to a changing culture. At the same time forms of worship need to be anchored in the unchanging biblical patterns of the worship of the people of God. Good liturgy is the key to this. Good liturgy is both flexible and anchored. It is ready to change in outward expression, such as the use of different styles of music, instruments, equipment, technology and so on. But the core of worship remains the same – to come into the presence of God, in spirit and in truth; and to seek his face, that in encountering the Lord Jesus Christ we may be healed, and saved, and transformed.

Jesus taught us to pray, 'Our Father in heaven.' God is our Father; we cry out to him, 'Abba [Daddy]! Father!' (Romans 8:15). Because Jesus has revealed God to be our loving heavenly Father, Christian worship will always have a dimension that is intimate and personal. But he is our Father in heaven. He is the transcendent God, the Lord God Almighty, creator of heaven and earth. So Christian worship must be clothed in reverence and awe. Like Moses, when we come into the presence of God, we should in a sense take off our shoes and remember that we are on holy ground. As we come before God, with hearts that are set on seeking his holy presence and knowing his power to transform, we shall find, as God's people have done across the ages, that he is faithful to his word, and that he will come to us, and reign in us, and through us transform the face of the earth.

The heart of Christian worship is a desire to seek the face of God, and to know him, more and more, each day of our lives. In the words of the prayer attributed to Richard of Chichester:

O most merciful Redeemer, Friend and Brother,
May I know thee more clearly
May I love thee more dearly
May I follow thee more nearly
Day by day.

8

A House of Prayer for All Nations

> Then he [Jesus] entered the temple and began to drive out those who were selling things there; and he said, 'It is written, "My house shall be a house of prayer"; but you have made it a den of robbers.' (Luke 19:45)

What did Jesus mean when he said, 'My house shall be a house of prayer'? Clearly he was deeply indignant and angry at the way in which the house of God, the temple, was being used as a place of buying and selling, and exploiting the poor, a 'den of robbers'. But he was also saying that the house of God is to be set aside for a holy purpose, to be a place of prayer. The quotation Jesus used is from Isaiah 56:7, 'My house shall be called a house of prayer for all peoples.' The phrase 'for all peoples' points to God's purpose in sending Jesus into the world. The kingdom of God that has broken through in Jesus Christ is not to be confined to a single temple or place of worship. In fact a new temple, not built by human hands, will enable Gentiles of all nations to worship God. That new temple is the Christian church, the body of all Christian believers. As 1 Peter 2:4–5 says, 'Come to him, a living stone, though rejected by mortals yet chosen and precious in God's sight, and like living stones, let yourselves be built into a spiritual house.'

So the church is called by God to be a house of prayer for all nations. Everything the church does in serving the community and in proclaiming the good news of Jesus in word and deed needs to be born out of worship and prayer. Our first call is to love God with all our hearts and minds and strength, and to invite others to do the same. We are primarily to be a house of prayer, to be dedicated to worship and prayer on society's behalf.

A prayerful church needs a leader who prays

When I first became Rector of the Church of the Ascension in Hilton, South Africa, I believed firmly in the importance of prayer. But I was very busy, and there was a lot to be done. So a daily time of prayer often, for one reason or another, did not find a place in my schedule. Sometimes I would realise that I needed time with God. So I would get into my car and drive to a quiet place away from my parish, and park beside a river, or find a quiet country church and spend two or three hours catching up with myself and with God. I needed 'time out' in order to bring my life and the things that were happening in our church to God in prayer.

However, after about five years at the Church of the Ascension I began to suffer symptoms of burn-out. I had simply been pushing myself too hard for too long. I was stressed and strained, and I knew something had to change. I was aware that I had been carrying too much of the burden for events that had taken place among our congregation. I had also felt that it was my personal responsibility to lead the church forward in mission and growth, and that I therefore had to set high standards for myself, and prove that I was capable of being a strong and competent church leader.

What I came to realise was that it was not my church at all. The church is the Lord's, and he is more than capable of ensuring its growth and vitality. God did not want me to transform the church; that is his business. What he asks of me is simply that I am faithful in prayer and in using the gifts he has given me to the best of my ability. He certainly does not expect me to become a workaholic for the sake of the kingdom of God. I came to realise that a good church leader is someone who models wholeness in Christ, in every aspect of life. This involves the spiritual, but it also involves leisure, physical health, good family relationships, and, of course, being faithful and responsible in doing the work of a pastor by caring for the flock.

Around this time I was encouraged to consider finding a spiritual director, someone I could see on a regular basis in order to talk about my prayer life. The person whom I began to see quickly shattered my illusions about prayer. I thought I would be talking about praying only. But he wanted to talk about anything important that was going on in my life. He pointed out to me that God is interested in the whole of my life, not just one or two 'spiritual' bits. So I soon accepted that when I went to see my spiritual director (normally once every two or three months) he would ask me a simple question: 'What's come up?' I would begin to tell him, and then he would help me to discern how God was at work in my life through the complex and often confusing events that make up the experience of human life.

This led to a major rethinking of my understanding of prayer and the ordering of my own private world before God. I realised that I could not lead a local church in my own strength. The ministry of the gospel of Jesus Christ is not possible for any human person apart from the grace of

God. I am utterly dependent on the daily sustaining and enabling mercy of the Lord Jesus Christ if I am to continue in this work. Truly, without him I can do nothing (John 15:5).

So I realised I would have to make a decision. I would put first things first, and that meant rooting the whole of my life and ministry in prayer. I decided that, from then on, *prayer would be the priority of my life*. I would never again be too busy to pray. If I had too much to do, something would simply have to be left undone. God would understand, because he had called me, first of all, to be a person of prayer.

Of course, in practice it has not been that easy. But that decision was a turning point. Since that time I have maintained a commitment to a daily time alone with God, except in times of illness or other pressing circumstances. But making prayer a priority means far more than a daily time of prayer. For me this has meant regular retreats and quiet days, an ongoing commitment to being accountable for my own heart and soul to a particular spiritual director, and a willingness to learn more about the classical spiritual disciplines and to put them into practice.

Time for God

Above all, our need is to make time for God.

> One thing I asked of the LORD,
>   that will I seek after:
> to live in the house of the LORD
>   all the days of my life,
> to behold the beauty of the LORD,
>   and to inquire in his temple. (Psalm 27:4)

The transforming church will be a church where prayer and making time for God are a clear priority. Unless we listen to

God, we shall not know what he is asking us to do. Being always comes before doing. I aim to be the kind of leader for whom this is clearly true in my own life. Only then can I hope to be a leader who enables others to be people of prayer, a people who have time for God.

Psalm 46:10 says, 'Be still, and know that I am God!' In order to listen to God we must first learn to be still. I am always impressed when I attend a church that has learnt to keep times of silence in the midst of its services. A church comfortable with silence, with reflection and waiting, is likely to be a church that listens. Such a church is also likely to be obedient to the voice of God.

Waiting and listening do not come easily to many people in our hectic, activity-centred world. Where do we look for security, for freedom from anxiety, in this 'material world'? How can we know, when we are struggling and life is throwing all kinds of tough things at us, that 'the victory is the Lord's'? Those who are most confident in the ultimate sovereignty of God and in his unfailing love and mercy are those who have learnt to wait upon God and to listen to him. In the discipline of stillness there comes a freedom from restlessness and anxiety. This is where we learn to be responsive not so much to our human needs and desires, but to the ultimate purposes and provision of God. He will not fail nor forsake us. But he calls his people to live by faith, not by sight. The leaders of God's people must be men and women of faith. The life of faith begins in the place apart, on my knees, alone before God. When I hear his voice and believe, and act as God has directed me, then I shall see things that are humanly speaking impossible, but possible with God. This is the key to the transforming power of the kingdom of God.

Worship opens the door for prayer. As the church takes seriously the call of God to seek his face, we find that his purpose is to make us a people of prayer. This means that prayer becomes central to the whole life of the church. Prayer takes place in services of worship, but it goes far beyond this. We need the daily discipline of prayer in individual lives, and the soaking of all the church's activities and initiatives in prayer. Beyond this lies a commitment to growth in the fullness of Christian spirituality and in all the spiritual disciplines of the church. Richard Foster's book *Celebration of Discipline* has reawakened for many people an interest in these disciplines, and a desire to deepen their own discipleship through them.[1]

These are the foundation of the life of prayer. Any church that is serious about prayer will be serious about these disciplines and will teach and encourage them.

The power of intercession

The movement of prayer in the church begins with private prayer, but it does not end there. It flows out to small groups of two and three, and to bigger groups of ten or twelve, meeting in homes or perhaps during lunch hours at work. The movement of prayer begins with tiny springs and little streams, which flow into one another and become a mighty river of intercession. Many people in our day are discovering anew the power of intercession.

I recently attended a Transformations prayer meeting in the city of Durban, South Africa. It was in a large church, on a weekday evening. The church was full; it was standing room only. The pews had been removed to enable more people to attend and to move around freely during the

---

[1] Richard Foster, *Celebration of Discipline* (London: Hodder & Stoughton, 1980).

meeting. There was singing and praise, followed by exhortation to continue to press forward in obedience to God's call for unity, reconciliation and fervent prayer in the city. And there was a great upsurge of prayer – aloud, vibrant, passionate and focused. I had experienced something similar in Cambridge just a few months previously. In many countries of the world a new transformation-centred movement of intercessory prayer is taking hold, even as I write. I am sure that this is highly significant for the future of the church in the twenty-first century.

Certainly in Durban I could see the connection between fervent united prayer and community transformation. A few days after the prayer meeting I attended, the following story appeared in the local daily newspaper, the *Natal Mercury*:

Mlaba Packs Christian Centre

The ANC's mayoral candidate for the metro's unicity, Mr Obed Mlaba, took his election campaign to the packed Durban Christian Centre in Berea Road yesterday, accompanied by his party's provincial leadership. Greeted by applause when he took the stage, Mr Mlaba promised that he, and a group of church leaders from the Durban area, had a plan to rid the city of crime and poverty and clean up its streets.

'We have had up to four meetings with 25 pastors, including pastor Vusi Dube of this church, and others in Durban where we discussed and came up with a plan to deal with crime and poverty in the city,' he said . . .

'For a long time we were oppressed by apartheid, but now we have democracy. Were it not for the contribution of the church, this freedom would not have been possible.'

In the *Transformations* video, George Otis Jr points to three primary factors responsible for transformed cities and communities in different parts of the world.

1. Persevering leadership (see Nehemiah 6:1–16).
2. Fervent, united prayer (see Jonah 3:5–10).
3. Social reconciliation (see Matthew 5:23–24; 18:15–20).

Of united prayer, George Otis Jr says:

> The second core factor in community transformation is fervent, united prayer. In each of our case studies, breakthroughs occurred when intercessors came together to address specific concerns. United prayer is a declaration to the heavenlies that a community of believers is prepared for divine partnership. When this welcoming intercession is joined by knowledge, it becomes focused – leading to and sustaining the kind of prayer that produces results.[1]

What is intercessory prayer?

Intercessory prayer happens when groups of people gather to seek God's face and to pray for the church and for the world. Intercession is essentially 'asking' prayer. We need to ask for those things that are according to God's will, and so first we need to be directed by the Holy Spirit as to how we pray. Corporate intercessory prayer is a deliberate coming together of God's people to pray, as led by the Holy Spirit, for the purposes of God to be accomplished in individual lives, in the church and in the world.

How does intercessory prayer happen? John Grove from York Diocese has written some helpful guidelines for organising an intercessory prayer meeting. He gives some suggestions of different ways of praying corporately:

---

[1] Quoted in *Beyond 2000 – Community Transformation*, SOMA, Cape Town, November 2000 (conference booklet).

- In groups of three or four or more, and in silence.
- In pairs, praying out loud.
- In silence.
- Open intercession in the whole group.
- Listening to God (ask for feedback and pray into these things in groups: perhaps one topic per group or, if there is one clear message which emerges, everyone can pray about that).
- 'Korean' style: everyone stands and prays out loud (English or tongues) at the same time for one topic. Fairly loud background music can help people to pray loudly without being able to hear themselves.
- 'YWAM' style: half the people sing while the other half pray, and then the halves change over.
- Using 'praise shouts' or other bits of liturgy.
- Sharing repentance in pairs and speaking God's forgiveness to one another.
- 'Korean Sandwich': as 'Korean' above but using a series of linked topics or biddings divided by a short chorus or song which everyone sings as the music swells and leads into it.

Many or all of these can be integrated into a half-hour or one-hour prayer session.[1]

When I was a student in South Africa I remember once visiting a missionary in the Transkei. I stayed in his house for a week, in the town of Butterworth. In the living room there was a large framed picture with the words, 'Prayer Changes Circumstances'. This missionary lived by faith, quite literally. That simple message on his living room wall has stayed with me. I have found, in my own experience, that this is true:

---

[1] *Anglicans for Renewal* magazine, Derby, autumn 2000.

prayer does change circumstances. But more than this: prayer changes me. Or perhaps I should say that I am changed through prayer. Our God is a God of change, of transformation. Prayer is the key to this.

I do not know how prayer works. I just know that it does. And I know why it works. We have a loving heavenly Father who cares for us, in every detail of our lives, and he has told us to pray to him, and to ask for things we need. Jesus said:

> Ask, and it will be given to you; seek, and you will find; knock, and it will be opened to you. For every one who asks receives, and he who seeks finds, and to him who knocks it will be opened. (Matthew 7:7–8).

Jesus has promised us that our heavenly Father hears the prayers of those who call to him. We do not have a complete understanding of God's ways, and the answers to our prayers are sometimes not what we would have wanted at the time. God deals with us according to his infinite mercy, goodness and love, and not according to our personal needs and desires. In prayer we enter into partnership with God in order to bring about his purposes in the world. But we must remember that he is always the senior partner.

God is in the business of transformation. His purpose is to transform our lives, our motives, attitudes and habits. Through a transformed people God is able to change communities, cities and nations. At the heart of all of this is prayer.

9

Holiness

Some years ago I came across a book by Jeremy Taylor entitled *The Rules and Exercises of Holy Living*. Jeremy Taylor was born in Cambridge in 1613, the son of a barber in the town. He entered Cauis College in Cambridge University at the age of 13, and after a distinguished academic course, took the degree of Master of Arts in 1633. He was ordained into the Anglican ministry at the age of 20 and soon attracted the attention of the archbishop, whose influence enabled him to become a fellow of All Souls, Oxford, in 1636. He served various parishes, finally becoming chaplain to King Charles I. After the royalist defeat in the civil war he was deprived of his parish, and he then wrote *The Rules and Exercises of Holy Living*, which was published in 1651. He later became Bishop of Down, Connor and Dromore in Ireland.

Taylor's book makes extraordinary and challenging reading for a Christian in Britain at the beginning of the twenty-first century. It seems that Jeremy Taylor's view of holiness is in many ways out of touch with the realities of life in our Western culture. For example, he writes in his 'Remedies Against Uncleanness':

Fly from all occasions, temptations, looseness of company, balls and revellings, indecent mixtures of wanton dancings, idle talk, private society with strange women, starings upon a beauteous face, the company of women that are singers, amorous gestures, garish and wanton dressings, feasts and liberty, banquets and perfumes, wine and strong drinks, which are made to persecute chastity, some of these being the very prologues to lust.

This gives us a taste of Jeremy Taylor's understanding of holy living. He was undoubtedly a holy man. But much of his teaching would today be viewed as puritanical and legalistic, even in the church. What then does holy living mean for the church now?

Holiness is a big problem for the church in the West. The prevailing culture says, 'You do your thing; I'll do mine.' Nobody has the right to tell anyone else what they should do in their own private world. 'This is the age of anything goes,' sang Sheryl Crow. It is the age of relativism. Moral absolutes are no longer a possibility for many people, in fact probably for the majority of people in Western Europe today. Yet the faith of the Bible and therefore of the Christian church is without doubt a faith rooted in moral absolutes. Those absolutes derive directly from the unchanging commandments of God to his people. He says, 'You shall be holy unto me, for I the Lord am holy.' He is the God of righteousness, and he expects his people to be righteous and holy. The problem is: what does this mean in the Western world at the beginning of the twenty-first century?

The liberal social philosophy that began to take hold in the 1960s has been extraordinarily influential in many nations, and its influence continues to spread. Most Islamic nations are still resisting it, as are a few other conservative or totalitarian societies. Some parts of the globe, such as large areas of north and central Africa, have not yet come under any significant

Western influence, but these areas are diminishing rapidly. Even Russia and China are both quickly becoming Western-ised, certainly in those areas opening up to Western economic development. The culture of Coca-Cola, McDonald's and Starbucks seems to have the world at its feet. And with it comes all the power and influence of the Western (mainly American) media and its liberal, relativistic philosophy.

Pierre Elliot Trudeau, the prime minister of Canada in the 1960s and 1980s, was one of the great political leaders of the second half of the twentieth century. He left an indelible mark on Canada, and his liberal philosophy has had a huge impact in making Canada the nation it is today. Trudeau's vision for Canada was a vision of tolerance and acceptance, a place where all Canadians, regardless of language, ethnic origin, education, family background or sexual orientation would have a place. Under his leadership, the laws on homosexuality were reformed, and Trudeau famously commented, 'The government has no place in the bedrooms of the nation.' Trudeau's view was that what is done in private is people's own private business. However, what is done in public is a different matter, and here the state may well have to intervene. Trudeau was a Christian, a committed Roman Catholic. He did not see morality and ethics as unimportant. For him, morality was in particular the concern of people of faith, including the church. The Christian church has to continue, even in a liberal society, to call all those who are followers and disciples of Jesus Christ to the highest standards of integrity and holiness, in response to the teaching and standards of Jesus himself.

But in practice the Christian church has found this exceptionally difficult. Mainline Protestantism has increasingly been secularised, and has largely adopted an acceptance and conformity to the spirit of the age. At best it has been playing catch-up. Many Protestant clergy and ministers, for example, now see marriage as merely an option for Christian couples who wish to live together, and would express no disapproval of those who choose not to marry, but who simply cohabit. The Western church has by and large been overwhelmed by the new liberal morality, and has little credible witness to a generation that knows no other way of thinking about human behaviour.

The power of the media

Having said this, the Roman Catholic Church, as well as a considerable number of smaller churches and church groupings, has tried to maintain a different set of standards, centred on the call of God in Christ to human society. Such churches have faced unyielding criticism and even vilification from the dominant liberal establishment in the West. They are often branded authoritarian, right wing and fundamentalist. The word 'fundamentalist' is one of the strongest, most emotive terms a liberal can use to denigrate someone they disagree with on moral or ethical issues.

The power of the Western media is awesome, and its reach is increasingly global. It is by no means morally or philosophically neutral, although the message it conveys varies from network to network, from movie to movie and so on. It would make no more sense simply to condemn all Western video and television output than to condemn all Western literature. But it is true to say that much of Western television, cinema, and the glossy print and news media is controlled by those who have a liberal moral philosophy. This philosophy is partly about tolerance and acceptance. But it is also very aware that sex sells, and the bottom line is all about profit. The net result is that much of Western society is obsessed with money, sex and power. This society is at the same time both wealthy beyond the wildest expectations of the immediate post-war generation, and yet profoundly morally confused, and even lost. So for those living in the Western world at the start of the twenty-first century, almost anything is possible, both materially and morally. There are few rules, and boundless possibilities. No wonder young people growing up in such a world are finding it difficult to work out what is the purpose of it all.

A world of brokenness

The statistics are horrendous. In the United States four out of ten girls are pregnant by the age of 20. Many of these are unplanned pregnancies, and most face the prospect of bringing up their child, or children, as a single parent. In Britain it is estimated that one woman in three will have had an abortion by the age of 45.

Everywhere I look today I see brokenness – broken marriages, broken lives, broken hearts. One of the saddest things is to see a young person, not even 21 years old, whose life has already been deeply scarred by the tragedy of abortion, drug abuse or alcoholism. In such a broken society the church faces an immense task as the agent of healing, a place of belonging, the signpost to a better way.

A young single mother with two small children started attending our church. She found a welcome and depth of care nothing in her life up to that point had prepared her for. She turned to Christ, and was baptised. At her baptism I asked her about her family. She pointed to the people of the congregation gathered around her. 'This is my family,' she said.

The church is called to be a new and distinctive community, a community that reflects not the values of the world and its kingdoms and power bases, but instead the values of the kingdom of God. That is a very great challenge for the church at the beginning of the new millennium. Yet for those who are serious about following Jesus Christ there are clear directions to be found in the words of Jesus himself. This is an age where Christian discipleship and holiness is a costly and unfashionable option. The way that leads to eternal life is narrow and difficult to find, as Jesus said it would be (Matthew 7:14). Yet many young people are willing to make such hard choices, and are looking for Christian leaders who will give them direction in these complex and demanding times.

I am increasingly persuaded that what is needed from the church and its leadership is not an accommodation of the secular relativist morality of our age, but a call to all those who would be Jesus' disciples to walk the way of the cross. This is the way of holiness, of self-denial, of obedience and sacrifice. This is the way that, in the promise of Jesus, leads to joy and fulfilment, and eternal life.

The life of Jesus

The way of Christ is the way of humility and righteousness, purity and reconciliation, mercy and obedience. Jesus said:

> Blessed are the poor in spirit, for theirs is the kingdom of heaven.
>
> Blessed are those who mourn, for they will be comforted.
>
> Blessed are the meek, for they will inherit the earth.
>
> Blessed are those who hunger and thirst for righteousness, for they will be filled.
>
> Blessed are the merciful, for they will receive mercy.
>
> Blessed are the pure in heart, for they will see God.
>
> Blessed are the peacemakers, for they will be called children of God.

Blessed are those who are persecuted for righteousness' sake, for theirs is the kingdom of heaven.

Blessed are you when people revile you and persecute you and utter all kinds of evil against you falsely on my account. Rejoice and be glad, for your reward is great in heaven, for in the same way they persecuted the prophets who were before you. (Matthew 5:2–12)

These words of Jesus, at the beginning of the Sermon on the Mount, are a wonderful summing up of what it truly means to be a follower of Christ. Holiness is primarily about character and integrity, about being true to who we are and to the one we believe in. Outward behaviour is a consequence of this. Holiness does not begin with morality; morality is a consequence of holiness.

So for Christians in a secular age the question is not 'What are the rules?' The question is rather 'What would Jesus do?' Paul says, in Colossians 3:17 (NKJV), 'And whatever you do in word or deed, do all in the name of the Lord Jesus, giving thanks to God the Father through Him.'

So the reason why, as Christians, we do not lie, steal or commit adultery is simply that such things are contrary to the way of Jesus. He is our Lord and Master; he is the way, the truth and life. He calls all those who are his disciples to live a particular life, which is a reflection of his own life and character. Our goal is to become Christlike, day by day. When we fail, we seek his forgiveness, and he gives us grace, again and again, to start anew. That is the meaning of Christian holiness.

Marching to a different drum

The word 'holy' means 'set apart'. That which is holy is given to God, set apart for his use and purpose. Holiness implies sacrifice and distinctiveness. So to be a holy people, the church will be distinctive. It will not easily fit in. As a result it may be unpopular or unfashionable. It may even be hated and persecuted. Certainly, the church will often be a small apparently insignificant group of people, swimming against the current and not, in the world's eyes, to be taken too seriously. We should not be surprised at this. Jesus never told his followers that they would be popular or fashionable.

Churches do not need to be popular, to attract huge numbers, or own large impressive buildings. There is nothing wrong with a vision for growth, or for seeing many people come to faith in Christ. But I don't recall Jesus saying anything about large buildings, except in his parable about the man who built bigger and bigger barns. He was called by Jesus a fool, because his central focus in life was on his wealth and material security, instead of on God. There will be times when the church is popular and receives favour from the government and the important people in society, and when large crowds will come to worship. But we know from the words of Jesus that we should be wary when all speak well of us (Luke 6:26). He warned his disciples that they would be persecuted and trampled upon, hated and betrayed. Ultimately what matters for Christians is not how popular we are or whether we have made a good impression, but whether or not we have been obedient to Jesus.

For Christians, holiness means being different, because it means being Christlike. It means living a different lifestyle, not ruled by materialism and busyness and pleasure-seeking, but ruled by Jesus. It means marching to a different drum, keeping in step with our own Master and Lord. It means being committed to purity and faithfulness, honesty and simplicity, in word and in deed. It means truth-telling and promise-keeping.

The character of Jesus is a servant character, marked by compassion and mercy. Jesus reached out constantly to those who were struggling, to the lost and lonely, the outcast and the sinner. The church does not stand in judgement upon those who do not live by the standards of Jesus. We simply call others to follow him, primarily by our lives rather than by our words. 'Preach the good news. If necessary use words,' said St Francis of Assisi. We reach out in love, as Jesus did, and we trust that he will touch many, as he has touched us, and as he has touched millions of others across the past 2,000 years.

For those of us who love Jesus and desire with our hearts to follow him, he asks of us nothing less than the whole of our lives. He sets us his own standards, and calls us to follow in his steps. So the church is right to exhort continually all those who call themselves 'Christian' to aim to live according to the highest standards of purity, faithfulness and righteousness.

Sex and marriage

As far as sex and marriage are concerned, the teaching of Jesus contradicts much popular thinking on the subject, certainly if most popular magazines and television soaps are anything to judge by. Jesus held a high view of marriage. For Jesus, marriage was a lifetime commitment between one man and one woman. Adultery was a falling short of the commandments of God and the demands of love and faithfulness to one's marriage partner. Divorce, according to Jesus, was allowed by Moses because of the hardness of the people's hearts, but, he said, in the beginning it was not so (Matthew 19:8). In other words, divorce is not what God intended to happen. The introduction to the marriage service in the Anglican Church states that marriage is a gift of God in creation, and a means of grace. God created man and woman, and marriage is the highest expression of love that is possible between a man and woman: total unconditional commitment to one another for the whole of their earthly life together.

The secular view of marriage is different. Polly Toynbee, in the *Radio Times* Christmas edition, December 1995, wrote:

> Recent research from socio-biologists and evolutionary psychologists suggests that humans are not made to be monogamous – and doesn't virtually all literature and experience tend towards that view, if we are honest? By teaching children to expect monogamy in their parents, and themselves, we set them up for disappointment. All around them are the children of separated parents, and yet we continue to hold above them this guilt-making ideal.
>
> We grow older, we change, we make mistakes, we change our partners. Serial monogamy, one partner at a time, but not the same person till death do us part – that seems to me a more natural pattern for us. The fact is the constraints of religion or Victorian morality have gone for good. If only we weren't always trying to squeeze our rumbustious natures into strait-jackets that don't fit, we might face the real problems and do something about them. Everyone is 'family' and putting it in capitals won't help us come to terms with social reality.

The church needs to have the courage to present, and hold on to, the biblical view of marriage. Of course marriages do sometimes break down, and sometimes divorce becomes inevitable. Marriages do go through both good and difficult times, and there is often a need for help, support and encouragement in order for a marriage to hold together. But for Christians marriage is a solemn lifetime vow, a covenant with God and one another. It is not to be considered in the same terms as any other legal contract. Marriage is a gift of God, and his will and purpose is that it should be a commitment for life, 'till death do us part'.

So the church must be careful not even to be seen to be buying into a 'serial monogamy' view of marriage. Rather it must hold on to a high view of marriage, as a great and glorious gift of God, full of rich and wonderful possibilities for love to grow and flourish, often over 40 or 50 or 60 years of married life together.

On many occasions I have been asked to take a funeral of an elderly man or woman, and have visited the surviving wife or husband. I have been able to say to them, 'In the midst of your loss, we can truly give thanks to God for all your years of married life and faithfulness to one another, for 40 or 50 or more years. What a wonderful achievement, so very special and significant, in so many ways!'

So too with sex before marriage, it is usually not helpful to say to young people, 'Thou shalt not . . .' Rather we can point them to seek God's plan for their future, and for many his purpose will be for their own blessing, fulfilment and happiness in a pure and holy marriage, becoming 'one flesh' with the one person with whom they will share the whole of their lives. Jesus said:

. . . 'For this reason a man shall leave his father and mother and be joined to his wife, and the two shall become one flesh'? So they are no longer two, but one flesh. Therefore what God has joined together, let no one separate. (Matthew 19:5–6)

This is a great ideal, and one worth investing in and waiting for. The biblical ideal of marriage in all its fullness is worth purity before marriage. Yet so often the church fails to communicate this, because we focus on rules and behaviour, rather than on all that flows to us from God through his transforming power at work in our hearts and lives. God is good, and he wants only to give good things to his children. We need to remember that the Bible unashamedly devotes an entire book to celebrating marital sex. But the Bible also sets boundaries, and rules, and warnings of the consequences for our own lives and families if we step outside those boundaries and break those rules. If we do this, we shall pay the price – we and those whose lives are linked with ours. God's desire is that no one should sin and fall short of his good and loving purposes for our lives. That is why he gives us such clear directions in the Bible. If we follow these instructions, we shall know the blessing and goodness of God in so many ways. That is his good and perfect will for us.

Money and giving

One of the greatest challenges to Christians in the West lies in our attitude to money and materialism. Jesus spoke very plainly to his disciples about this issue: 'No one can serve two masters . . . You cannot serve God and wealth' (Matthew 6:24).

We have to make a choice. Who are we going to serve? As Bob Dylan once sang, 'You gotta serve somebody.' Will it be God or money? Who will be our master?

For Christians, clearly our response must be that we shall serve the Lord, and put him first. But in an affluent and materialistic society, how in practice do we do this? The key is to make sure that our God is the Lord. Money must never take control of our lives. One of the best ways to ensure that our wealth does not take hold of our hearts is by letting go of it whenever it comes our way. We do this by giving.

Giving is a core Christian discipline. Just as our God is a God who gives, who has given even his own Son for us, so we are to be a giving people. When we have truly experienced the grace and generosity of God we shall become truly generous people. We shall be generous with our time and energy, and shall be generous with our money. We cannot give our hearts to God unless we also give him our pockets (or perhaps our credit cards). Giving is a key part of our response to the gospel, the self-giving love of God for us in Jesus Christ.

The church today needs a theology of generosity, which will place all discussion of material wealth in the context of God's amazing gift of his love and salvation in Jesus. This means that our understanding of the church begins by saying that the church exists to give praise and thanks to God for all his gifts to us, and to give to others as he has given to us.

It is important for us to face the fact that money has become a primary issue, and possibly the primary issue, for modern society. We are obsessed by money. It seems increasingly that political and social policy in the developed nations is determined by economics and economists. The power of big business, of market forces and institutional investors, is enormous. These are probably the most powerful forces in Western society today.

Christian faith, however, proclaims the true meaning of our life and existence on earth. We are not here primarily to create wealth. We are here to glorify God and to live generously for the sake of the gospel. Jesus said, 'Freely you have received, freely give' (Matthew 10:8 NKJV). We are what and how we give.

Our giving should always flow from and express our gratitude to God. Everything we have is his. We are simply stewards or caretakers. We can only give to him that which he has already given to us. St Anselm said, 'When you give alms you do not bestow a bounty; you pay a debt.'

Clearly God calls us to use and to enjoy those things he has given us. But we are also to give away some of what we have been given, and our giving should always involve a sacrificial element. This is where a proportion comes in. To give a tithe is to give God the 'first-fruits' of all we receive, as an acknowledgement that everything in fact belongs to him, and that he is the provider of all our needs. And a tithe, or 10 per cent, for many of us will only be the beginning. The exact amount we give, as our tithe, will vary from individual to individual. But the principle is clear. God calls his people to be a generous, giving people, as he himself is infinitely generous.

In this age of materialism we can give powerful testimony to our self-giving God by being a consistently generous people, by freely giving and freely serving. We seek to model a new society built not on accumulation but on giving. Wealth itself is not sinful or wrong; it becomes a problem only when it is not accompanied by generosity. There is great freedom and joy in regularly learning to de-accumulate; in other words to give away the things we don't need, or even that we do need, but that other people such as the homeless and the hungry also need. What about those clothes hanging in our wardrobes, and those books unread upon our shelves? What about the money sitting in our bank accounts? What does the love of Christ ask, even require of us, especially those of us who have so much? 'Simplify, simplify' is the call of the Holy Spirit to Christians in the rich developed world. Learn to give it away, and become free to trust the poor, and to trust God, without constantly wanting to protect and look after our worldly wealth.

We need to take seriously the words of Jesus about wealth. To the rich young ruler he said, 'If you would be perfect, go, sell what you possess and give to the poor, and you will have treasure in heaven; and come, follow me' (Matthew 19:21 RSV).

In the Sermon on the Mount he said:

Do not store up for yourselves treasures on earth, where moth and rust consume and where thieves break in and steal; but store up for yourselves treasures in heaven . . . For where your treasure is, there your heart will be also. (Matthew 6:19–21)

In the words of St Francis of Assisi:

We must not think the utility and value of coin or money is greater than that of stones. The devil wants to bind those who do desire and value it more. And so let us who have left all things beware, lest for so little we lose the Kingdom of heaven.

Be transformed

Do not be conformed to this world, but be transformed by the renewing of your minds, so that you may discern what is the will of God – what is good and acceptable and perfect. (Romans 12:2)

This is Paul's challenge for the church in our time too. The Western church has lost its cutting edge, and needs to rediscover a prophetic holiness, in word and deed. In this it may be able to learn from the example of the church in other times and other societies, where the church, or even a faithful remnant within the church, has taken on a prophetic minority role. There have been many periods in church history where the church has been called to speak and live for Christ in conditions of weakness and personal danger. The 'Confessing Church' in Nazi Germany found itself in such a position. Dietrich Bonhoeffer is well known for his book *The Cost of Discipleship*, in which he draws a distinction between cheap grace and costly grace. Bonhoeffer says, 'Cheap grace is the deadly enemy of our church. We are fighting today for costly grace.' Cheap grace seeks forgiveness and solace without the demands of prophetic obedience. Costly grace is rooted in living out the demands of the gospel, even at great personal cost.

Bonhoeffer also wrote *Life Together*, a book less well known than *The Cost of Discipleship*, but in its way as important. It describes the life of a Christian community, seeking to be obedient to Christ in prayer, fellowship, worship and ministry. *Life Together* was written in the context of Germany between 1935 and 1938, when Bonhoeffer was called by the Confessing Church to take charge of an illegal, clandestine seminary for the training of young pastors.

Bonhoeffer taught that a Christian's allegiance is to Christ and the church, and not to this world and its demands and pleasures. He writes:

The member of the Body of Christ has been delivered from the world and called out of it. He must give the world a visible proof of his calling, not only by sharing in the church's worship and discipline, but also through the new fellowship of brotherly living. Where the world seeks gain, the Christian will renounce it. Where the world exploits, he will dispossess himself, and where the world oppresses, he will stoop down and raise up the oppressed. If the world refuses justice, the Christian will pursue mercy, and if the world takes refuge in lies, he will open his mouth for the dumb, and bear testimony to the truth.[1]

---

[1] D. Bonhoeffer, *The Cost of Discipleship* (London: SCM Press, 1988).

But Bonhoeffer did not believe that Christians should simply withdraw from the world, and aim to live holy and unpolluted lives in isolated communities, separated from the rest of society. Jesus prayed that the Father would not take his disciples out of the world, but that he would keep them from the evil one (John 1:7–15). So Bonhoeffer writes:

> Let the Christian remain in the world, not because of the good gifts of creation, nor because of his responsibility for the course of the world, but for the sake of the Body of the incarnate Christ and for the sake of the church. Let him remain in the world to engage in frontal assault on it, and let him live the life of his secular calling in order to show himself as a stranger in this world all the more. But that is only possible if we are visible members of the Church. The antithesis between the world and the Church must be borne out in the world. That was the purpose of the incarnation.[1]

---

[1] *Ibid.*

Conclusion

Future church

The conventional church of the twentieth century is dying. Its time has passed. We now live in a new century and a new millennium. What will the church of the future look like?

Clearly there will be many different models of the future church. But a recovery of key principles and values seems to me to be essential if the church in the West is to make any significant impact in the new century. In this book I have described my understanding of the church as an agent of transformation. That is the church I believe in. It is a church which exists to proclaim in word and deed the good news of the kingdom of God. It is a church that changes society and the world.

I have said also that the primary purpose of the church in the West at this time is to create community with Christ at the centre. Christianity in the twenty-first century is primarily relational. I am convinced that it will be through belonging and through relationships rooted in the love and mercy of God that this generation will come to know Christ. For this generation belonging leads to believing, and only then to behaving in a more Christian way.

In our church in Cambridge, we have recently revised our Sunday worship programme. For some years a growing number of teenagers and young adults have been attending our Sunday morning service. This service had until a few years ago been a fairly traditional family service, with a large number of children and young families as well as a number of older retired people who have been part of the church for many years. We wanted to encourage the teenagers to feel that they belonged and were valued as members of the church. We increasingly gave them a significant stake in the planning and leading of the morning service. However, this meant that more and more of the music at the morning service reflected the taste of the young people in our church. The older members of the congregation did not always find this easy to cope with. 'Please can we have some more hymns?' was a request that I often heard. Finally we came to the point where we realised that there was a need to start a new congregation, geared primarily to the teenagers and young adults. This now meets every Sunday at 7 pm. The service is very informal, the music is fairly loud and afterwards there is hot chocolate and doughnuts. Many young people are coming, and they love to hang around after the service. Often they don't go home until after 11 pm.

Our goal is to enable young people in our community to come to know the love and power of God in and through Jesus. This has meant rethinking a lot of the ways that we 'do' church. We have to ask, in everything we do, 'Is it accessible?' Most young people in our community have little or no previous experience of church. We need to speak to them in a language they understand, and first and foremost that means unconditional acceptance and welcome.

In an earlier chapter I wrote about my visit to Langley Vineyard, near Vancouver in Canada. Since then I have visited a number of other churches with similar values and styles of worship. Langley Vineyard has a website entitled FLV – Friends Langley Vineyard. This is what it says:

Welcome to the digital home of Friends Langley Vineyard Church.

Who are we? We are friends and neighbours of all ages, all financial means, all potentials, all experiences. We are simple and complex. We are a community focused on presenting the mystery of Christ and sharing the tools needed to unwrap that. We long to experience the Almighty . . . not just on Sunday but during every moment of our lives. At the altar, at play, at home, at work . . . to experience Christ and feel his holy breath in our beings.

We have vowed to leave behind all of the things that hold us back from our goal. Our finish line is well defined: we want to be with God. What do we value? That's easy:

- We value evangelism through relationship.
- We value lifestyle discipleship through relationship.
- We value leadership development.
- We value the obvious ministry of the Holy Spirit.
- We value worship as a lifestyle of responsiveness and extravagant love towards God.
- We value generosity as a lifestyle of extravagant giving in time, energy, and money.
- We value a servant heart.

Why Friends? Friendship is our highest value. It's what we long for more than anything – friendship with God and friendship with each other.

This is one example of future church, a church where friendship and relationship with God and with one another is central to everything that happens. So for many of this generation future church is likely to be an informal, worship-centred, open and accepting group of people with little denominational awareness. Their music is contemporary. Their desire is to experience the Almighty and to share their lives with one another in relationships of depth, commitment and generosity.

But if this new model of church becomes focused only upon fulfilling the needs of its own members, its impact on the world of the twenty-first century will be very limited. This is the age of informality and 'friends', but it is also the age of globalisation and consumerism. Without a prophetic cutting edge and a transformed model of discipleship, the church in the developed world will continue to decline. In Britain, and in much of the affluent West, we live in a culture that consumes voraciously, and then conveniently insulates itself from the people upon whom it depends to make the goods and grow the food we consume. So it is vitally important to look for models of being church in the twenty-first century that address the issues of globalisation and challenge our Western preconceptions and self-indulgence.

In Chapter 1 I wrote about Peter Kerchhoff and his work with PACSA in South Africa. South Africa in the twenty-first century is facing new challenges, and PACSA continues to be active in working for a vision of God's justice, love and hope in that nation. In May 1999, at a celebration of the twentieth year of PACSA, Chris Langeveld spoke of how PACSA's pilgrimage of faith has contributed to understanding some of the elements of what being church in Africa entails:

- Prophetic action which denounces injustice in its many forms and announces signs of new life and liberation.

- A spirituality of healing which seeks to deal with the legacy of violence and abuse that infects our social relations.
- A life of prayer which retrieves a sense of the mystical to challenge the banality and crass materialism of an invasive market culture.
- A restoration of the full dignity and role of women in the structures of church and society.[1]

Unless the church in the West hears and embraces these and other prophetic insights, it will remain a feeble and insular club with little hope of bringing transformation and healing to society and to the world.

But if . . . If the future church in the West can find a new voice within the postmodern culture of our time, and cry out for justice, for compassion and for true spirituality . . . If the future church can create community with Christ at the centre, across the nation, in the inner cities and suburbs, in the villages and farming communities, and even among the homeless and the disenchanted youth . . . If the future church can recover a model of Christian discipleship that calls women and men everywhere to change their way of thinking and lay down their lives in following Jesus and making known his salvation . . . If the future church is known by all people to be made up of those who serve the poor and care for the lost and broken-hearted people of our consumerist and self-indulgent age . . .

THEN there will be a transforming future church, which God will use to transform the face of the earth, that his kingdom may come and his will be done on earth as it is in heaven.

---

[1] PACSA Annual Report 1999.

Other books in the Futurechurch *series include:*

Shapes of the Church to Come
by Michael Nazir-Ali

'Rooted in Scripture and forged in pastoral practice, the key insights in this book address global and local issues that must not be ignored if the church is to stay alive and relevant.'(David Coffey, President, Baptist Union)

Communication that Connects
by David Beer

Having a message to proclaim may not be unique, but believing it is for everyone is definitely counter-cultural. This book will help leaders, preachers and those who share their faith to proclaim a no-compromise message in culturally relevant ways.

Leadership Tool Kit
by Bryn Hughes

After nearly twenty years in management training, Bryn Hughes is convinced that enhancing the skills of leadership is critical for ministers of churches, leaders of missions and other Christian organisations. These skills come into sharp focus when training the crucial second tier of leadership.

*FUTURE*CHURCH ◆